MEDIA AND MENTAL DISTRESS

Glasgow Media Group

edited by
Greg Philo

LONGMAN
London and New York

Addison Wesley Longman Limited,
Edinburgh Gate, Harlow, Essex
CM20 2JE, England
and Associated Companies throughout the world.

Published in the United States of America
by Addison Wesley Longman Inc., New York

First published 1996

ISBN 0 582 29219 0   PPR

British Library Cataloguing-in-Publication Data

A catalogue record for this book is
available from the British Library

Library of Congress Cataloging-in-Publication Data

Media and mental distress / edited by Greg Philo ; Glasgow Media Group.
    p. cm.
    Includes bibliographical references and index.
    ISBN 0–582–29219–0 (alk. paper)
    1. Mental illness in mass media.   2. Mass media—Social aspects.
  I. Philo, Greg. II. Glasgow University Media Group.
P96.M45M43 1996
362.2—dc20   96–9069
                                             CIP

Set by 8 in 10/11 pt Palatino
Printed and Bound by Antony Rowe Ltd, Eastbourne
Transferred to digital print on demand, 2002

A lot of things you read in the papers and they've been diagnosed as being schizophrenic. These murderers – say Donald Neilson, was he no schizophrenic? – the Yorkshire Ripper ... in *Brookside* that man who is the child-abuser and the wife-beater – he looks like a schizophrenic – he's like a split personality, like two different people. (Audience group member, Motherwell)

The actual people I met weren't violent – that I think they are violent, that comes from television, from plays and things. That's the strange thing – the people were mainly geriatric – it wasn't the people you hear of on television. Not all of them were old, some of them were younger. None of them were violent – but I remember being scared of them, because it was a mental hospital – it's not a very good attitude to have but it is the way things come across on TV and films – you know, mental axe murderers and plays and things – the people I met weren't like that, but that is what I associate them with. (Audience group member, Glasgow)

When I was told I was schizophrenic, I was very intimidated by it – I thought I was some sort of monster. I didn't actually feel like a monster, but when they said I was schizophrenic, I just couldn't believe it ... It's just such a hell of a word, you know and it's got a hell of a stigma ... My window cleaner asked me 'would you not hit me over the head with the hammer?' – I had to reassure him that 'look mate, I'm not violent' and he was telling the neighbours. It rots you, it just rots you. (User of services, Glasgow)

Contents

Acknowledgements

Our thanks are due to all those who have helped in this project. Thanks especially to Lisa Beattie, Kathleen Ward and Joanne Yuill for their help in preparing the manuscript. Other members of the Glasgow Media Group also deserve special thanks: John Eldridge, Jenny Kitzinger, David Miller, Jacquie Reilly, Kevin Williams, Peter Beharrell and Cathie Irvine. Thanks also to Marilyn Hall and Eve and Marilyn Maine. For help in recording programmes and data collection thanks very much to Claire Heard, Sarah Williams, Justine Rothwell, Dawn Rowley and Rick Holliman. We would like also to thank the following organisations for their help and support, The Health Education Board for Scotland, The Scottish Association for Mental Health, MIND and The Royal College of Psychiatrists. Thanks especially to Mike Shooter, Deborah Hart, Bryce Pitt, Jim Dyer, Anthony Clare, Liz Sayce, Helen Storey and Claire Walker. For further support we would like to thank Robert Beattie of IBM Scotland, Penumbra, and other members of the Scottish Mental Health Working Group. Thanks also to all our friends in television and the press who helped us with interviews and contacts.

A very personal thanks is due to Mary Philo, John Philo and Sarah Philo for putting up with the disruption caused by a grumpy academic relative. We would also like to thank Sarah Caro and Lynette Miller of Addison Wesley Longman and Jenny Roberts, whose support through the process of producing this book has been invaluable. There are very many other academics, colleagues and friends who have been a source of advice and cheerful help along the way. Thanks to all of you.

We are grateful to the following for permission to reproduce copyright material: Caledonian Newspapers Limited for a headline from the *Evening Times*, 14th May 1993; Daily Sport for a headline from the *Daily Sport*, 6th April 1993; Mirror Group Newspapers Limited for headlines from the *Daily Mirror*, 4th May 1993 and 16th April, 1993; News Group Newspapers for a cartoon from *The Sun*, 18th March 1993.

Contributors

David Crepaz-Keay is Chair of Survivors Speak Out.

Lesley Henderson is a Researcher at Glasgow University Media Unit.

Greg McLaughlin is a Lecturer in media at University of Coleraine.

Greg Philo is Research Director at Glasgow University Media Unit and Reader in Sociology at the University of Glasgow.

Stephen Platt is Research Director at the Research Unit for Health and Behavioural Change at the University of Edinburgh.

Jenny Secker is Research and Development Officer at the Health Education Board for Scotland.

Introduction

This volume brings together the most recent work by the Glasgow Media Group in the area of the media and mental health/illness. The research examines the content of media images and shows how conditions such as schizophrenia are portrayed and routinely stigmatised. The research also illustrates the impact of such images on public belief and on the attitudes and responses of carers, as well as on those of users of mental health services. These issues also have a profound importance for questions of social policy, particularly in relation to programmes such as Community Care. Our research was originally developed in conjunction with the Health Education Board for Scotland and has now been further developed through contacts with other professional bodies such as the Royal College of Psychiatrists and organisations of users of services such as Survivors Speak Out.

In the first chapter Stephen Platt and Jenny Secker examine past research about public attitudes to mental health issues and the part played by the media in shaping these, and the significance of such research for key areas of health and social policy. They highlight a number of limitations concerning both the content of this previous research and the methods which have been used. They note that very little research examining media content appears to have been undertaken in Britain, and it clearly cannot be assumed that the findings of North American research are relevant to the British context. Those studies which have attempted to relate media content to attitudes have been limited to examining the short-term influence of particular films and television series, or of press coverage of specific events. In addition, the reliance of these studies on quantitative research designs and techniques means they have been unable to address the complex processes involved in belief formation and in the interpretation of media messages.

The research in this volume is an attempt to examine systematically the way in which the British media deal with mental health issues. By using qualitative methods we are exploring the cumulative, longer term influence of media content and the processes involved in the formation of beliefs and attitudes. Where mental health is concerned, the development of knowledge about the part played by the media in shaping beliefs and attitudes is not simply of academic interest. In particular we are concerned with the significance of our research for the development of community care for people with mental health problems. We suggest that constructive attitudes on the part of local communities are essential for the success of this policy. There are other problems, of course, with the community care programme apart from media representations. The need for proper resourcing of the programme has frequently been commented upon. We also recognise that the media are not simply inventing stories about violence attributed to the mentally ill. There have been tragic cases involving extreme violence and death. But our view is that the media are highlighting a tiny minority of cases relative to the very large number of people with mental health problems, and that in doing so media accounts are distorting public perceptions of the whole area of mental health. As Liz Sayce of MIND has written: 'it appears that irrespective of the facts, the myth of growing patient violence has taken a firm hold' (Sayce 1995b: 132). In this sense the influence of the media is a serious obstacle for organisations attempting to provide community-based resources.

In the second chapter, Lesley Henderson analyses the production processes which condition media images in both factual and fictional programmes. Her work is based on interviews with journalists and makers of factual programming, as well as with production teams for fictional programmes such as *Brookside* and other soap operas. In these, she explores the pressures which exist on journalists, writers and producers to make programmes within very tightly defined limits on what is deemed to have strong news or entertainment value.

In Chapter 3 David Crepaz-Keay of Survivors Speak Out analyses media coverage of the Boyd Confidential Inquiry. This inquiry into homicides and suicides directed by Dr William Boyd produced *A Preliminary Report on Homicide*, which was published in August 1994. The report showed what many in the mental health field already knew: that murders by people diagnosed mentally ill were extremely rare, and that the characteristics of both perpetrator and victim were remarkably similar to those of any homicide drawn at random. The analysis provided on these cases in the report destroyed many of the myths of the 'psycho killer', but few reporters appeared to notice this. Only two of the 22 victims were unknown to their assailant, making the image of the random killing far from the truth. The findings of the inquiry could have blown away myths but instead were used to reinforce stereotypes because what was a good report was so badly reported.

Chapter 4 presents the research on media content, which has been produced by the Glasgow Media Group. This consisted of a content analysis of coverage of mental health/illness over a period of one month. For television, we recorded the main evening news bulletins as well as the children's programme *News Round* plus samples of local television news magazines and current affairs and documentary programmes whenever they were appropriate. For the press, we analysed the output of eight national newspapers plus samples of local press 10 women's magazines and some children's publications. This was a very extensive sample and the purpose of the analysis was to identify the dominant messages which were given on mental illness across a variety of media. The techniques of content analysis which were used here are designed to identify the heaviest carriers of meaning in non-fictional texts. We show, for example, the range of themes which are present in news stories, and highlight crucial elements of language and visual images which are likely to have the most impact on audiences. Our earlier research has suggested that such language and imagery can have a crucial influence in forming ways of understanding and the development of social attitudes.

In the case of news stories we looked at the use of headlines and different types of news language, at how central characters in stories were labelled as 'mentally ill' and the types of actions with which they were associated. In practice the sample yielded a very large number of items, 562 in all relating to mental health/illness. Their content fell into five main categories: (1) violence to others; (2) harm to self; (3) prescriptive/treatment/recovery issues; (4) criticism of accepted definitions of mental illness; (5) comic images. Of these categories, violence to others was by far the most common type of coverage, outweighing the next most common (category 3) by a ratio of 4 to 1. Such a count actually overestimates the presence of positive images since category 3 was largely composed of letters to problem pages and advice columns. By contrast the negative images are more likely to be highlighted for their dramatic impact.

We also analysed the range of themes which are present in soap operas and other fictional accounts. These included *Coronation Street*, *Brookside*, *EastEnders*, *Neighbours*, *Home and Away* and Scottish Television's *Take the High Road*. We also analysed three medical drama series, *Casualty*, *Medics* and *Children's Ward*, as well as relevant single dramas and films. In addition we examined children's programmes, including the Saturday morning magazines, for their cartoons, feature items and live entertainment spots. In analysing the fictional material we looked at key storylines relating to mental illness, and at the structure of plots and dramatic action. We show the manner in which these can promote attitudes and generate affective reactions among the audience towards central characters of the drama. The structure of the plot and relations between characters in most soap operas establish very quickly who are to be seen as 'villains' to be reviled and who are meant to elicit our sympathy. In the next chapter we show how the construction of fictional characters in soap operas, as well as films and other drama, can have a profound impact upon audience belief.

Chapter 5 focuses on the audience reception studies undertaken by the Media Group. This analysis used focus groups drawn from the general population, who were asked to work through a programme of exercises and interviews. In the exercises, sub-groups of two or three people were asked to write news reports prompted by copies of original headlines from the newspapers. They were also asked to write dialogue for an episode of ITV's *Coronation Street*, prompted by still photographs from the programme. Following this, each member of the group gave written replies to questions. In writing their own stories, the audience group demonstrated a remarkable ability to reproduce the style and language of television news and the press. We also found that some group members could reproduce detailed and accurate scripts from the soap opera *Coronation Street*, months after the relevant scenes had been transmitted. In this case the photographs which were used related to a storyline in which a mentally ill person had an erotic fixation on the husband of one of the regular characters. These scenes had apparently generated an intense hostility towards the mentally ill character among the majority of the group members who had seen them. A much smaller number suggested that she needed psychiatric help – a judgement which was formed mostly on the basis of their own professional or personal experience in the area.

One of the key issues explored in this research was whether conditions such as schizophrenia were believed to be associated with violence. Forty per cent of the people in the audience sample believed this to be so, giving the media as the source of their beliefs. We also found, unusually, that the power of media images had apparently been so great that beliefs derived from the media could overwhelm knowledge which came from direct experience. Chapter 5 provides evidence of the influence which media can have upon audience belief. Television and the press are clearly very important sources of information and can generate strong emotional responses in viewers and readers. Some of the messages about violence and mental illness exploit deep anxieties about the unknown and unpredictable in what is seen as a very frightening world. At the same time other images can relate to and develop quite different responses to the need for care and sympathy for people who are seen as helpless victims. It is quite possible for both of these cultural elements to co-exist in people's consciousness. But the depth of anxiety is so great in this area that some media accounts can evidently exert great power.

Our final chapter is based on interviews with mental health professionals, carers and users of mental health services. It examines how stigmatising media images can affect the attitudes of carers as well as the self-definition of those who are mentally distressed. There are crucial links which we begin to examine between media images, family and neighbourhood attitudes and processes of recovery. We draw conclusions in a number of areas. First, we relate our research to current debates on media influence and the power of messages. There is now an extensive literature which has promoted the concept of the 'active' audience. Much of this work is based on methodologies which have effectively 'bracketed off' the question of media influence. There is no doubt that this work has distracted attention from key issues on the power and impact of media messages. Our new research provides very strong evidence to question many current assumptions in communications and cultural studies about the ability of audiences to negotiate and reject dominant structures of meaning.

Finally, we turn to the relevance of this research for current media practice and to how this could be improved. The Health Education Board for Scotland, in conjunction with the NUJ, has already published guidelines for journalists. The Royal College of Psychiatrists has recently added its voice by calling for a national debate on media coverage and how it affects distressed people, carers and their families. We hope that this volume will make a major contribution to this debate.

CHAPTER 1

Why media images matter

Jenny Secker and Stephen Platt

The research we describe in this book is concerned with the ways in which the British mass media portray mental illness. We examine the content of media images and illustrate their impact on public beliefs, on the feelings and experiences of mental health service users and on the attitudes and responses of carers. The purpose of this chapter is to provide some contextual information in order to establish the significance of the research. We begin by assessing the importance of media images for key areas of public policy and for journalists and broadcasters themselves. Systematic research can also support policy development by providing evidence to underpin arguments for change. In the second section of the chapter, we therefore review previous research into public attitudes and the impact of the media in order to explain the contribution we wish our own research to make.

The importance of media images

It is recognised that the media have a positive part to play in encouraging attitudes which are conducive to good health (Scottish Office 1991, Department of Health 1992). Where mental health is concerned, however, fears that media impact is largely negative are widespread. In this section we place these concerns in context by examining the implications for two key areas of public policy: the move from institutionalised care in psychiatric hospitals towards care in the community for people diagnosed mentally ill; and the increasing emphasis of health policies on health promotion and prevention, as opposed to the treatment of illness. In addition, we explore the implications for journalists and broadcasters who are themselves concerned with fair and accurate reporting.

Community care

Since publication of the White Paper *Better Services for the Mentally Ill* in 1975, it has been the policy of successive British governments to encourage the development of locally based health and social services to meet the needs of people diagnosed mentally ill. By the end of the 1980s, however, it was recognised that progress had not been uniformly satisfactory. In 1989 the government therefore published a second White Paper, *Caring for People: Community Care in the Next Decade and Beyond* (Department of Health 1989). The stated aim was to secure the delivery of good quality local services by clarifying roles and responsibilities, bringing together the relevant sources of finance and improving accountability. Throughout *Caring for People*, the emphasis is on providing a better quality of life than is possible in large, often remote psychiatric hospitals in order to ensure that people diagnosed mentally ill are able to achieve their full potential.

Whether implementation of the community care policies set out in the White Paper is succeeding in achieving these aims is a matter of ongoing debate, largely because of questions about the adequacy of the resources available. For example, McCollam (1992) argued on the basis of her analysis of the community care plans for 15 areas of Scotland that the transfer of resources from hospitals to the community was a major obstacle to change which arrangements for bridging finance had failed to overcome. Two years later, in their submissions to the Scottish Affairs Committee Inquiry into the effect of hospital closures both the Royal College of Psychiatrists and the Royal College of Nursing argued similarly that the loss of acute hospital beds was resulting in patients being discharged while still seriously ill and that, once discharged, patients were receiving inadequate care (Scottish Affairs Committee 1995). These views have been echoed by both the Mental Welfare Commission for Scotland (1994) and the Mental Health Act Commission in England (1993), while further concerns have been expressed about increased suicide rates among people discharged from hospital (Goldacre *et al.* 1993).

On the other hand, evidence also exists to support the claim that some community care initiatives do achieve their aims. Where studies have employed measures of health and quality of life to assess the impact on long-term hospital patients of moving to community-based accommodation, these have demonstrated that people's quality of life can improve significantly in terms of factors such as their physical environment, degree of freedom and relationships with staff (Simic *et al.* 1992, Barry 1993, Thornicroft *et al.* 1992). Qualitative studies designed to explore service users' perceptions in greater depth have also produced similar findings, suggesting that these are not simply an artifact of the standardised measures used by other researchers (Petch 1990, Powell 1993).

If implemented properly, then, it appears that community care policies can be successful. In addition to the problem of inadequate resources, however, it is becoming apparent that hostile public attitudes can be a major obstacle to success. In Scotland, attempts by local residents to block supported accommodation projects have been documented by the Scottish Association for Mental Health (1992), and in one case an objection prompted the Scottish Office to review their guidance to health boards regarding consultation with neighbours. Had this objection succeeded, it would have placed the development of community care in jeopardy by giving local residents the right to choose their neighbours (Scottish Mental Health Forum 1992). In England too, attempts to block local projects have been well documented both by the popular press, and by specialist journals (*Community Care* 1993, *Health Service Journal* 1992).

While much of this reporting is factual and non-partisan, concern is growing among those involved in community care about the impact of other media coverage. For example, Vousden (1989) argues that the use by the tabloid press of words such as 'loony' and 'maniac' to describe the perpetrators of violent crime is likely to provoke public fears about people diagnosed mentally ill. Equally, he takes issue with other journalists' use of the term 'schizophrenic' to signify ambivalence or division, on the grounds that this perpetuates the myth of schizophrenia as 'split personality'.

In view of the widespread publicity surrounding a number of recent tragedies, it might seem reasonable to assume that media images of the type highlighted by Vousden simply reflect the justified fears of the public about the risk of random violence on the part of people diagnosed mentally ill. However, research in the United States has shown that mental illness is not a reliable predictor of violence and that the vast majority of people diagnosed mentally ill are never aggressive towards others (Monahan 1992). These findings are supported in Britain by the Steering Committee of the Confidential Inquiry into Homicides and Suicides by Mentally Ill People (1996), established by the Department of Health (media coverage of their preliminary report of 1994 is discussed in Chapter 3 of this volume). In their 1996 report, the committee conclude that the kind of random violence feared by the public and given a high profile by the media is a rare occurrence, accounting for only 3 of the 39 cases examined over a period of two years. In the remaining 36 cases, the victim was known to the assailant, being most commonly a family member. As the report also points out, all 39 cases account for only a small proportion of the total number of the 500 homicide convictions obtained on average each year in Britain. Given these facts, it seems there is justifiable cause for concern not only about the part played by the media in fuelling unjustified fears, but also about the potential impact on community care policies. As the policy director of the National Association for Mental Health (MIND) has put it, there is a real danger that new policies based not on a proper examination of the risks, but on a knee-jerk response to ill-considered fears, will undermine the principle of community care and leave a legacy lasting many years (Sayce 1995a).

Health promotion

Alongside the development of community care, an increasing emphasis on the promotion of health and prevention of illness has been evident in health policy, both in Britain and elsewhere, since the mid-1980s. At the European level, the World Health Organisation's 'Health for All' policy sets out a target for mental health which focuses mainly on the prevention of illness and suicide, but which also encompasses health promotion in terms of improving the quality of life of people diagnosed mentally ill: 'By the year 2000, there should be a sustained and continuing reduction in the prevalence of mental disorders, an improvement in the quality of life of all people with such disorders, and a reversal of the rising trends in suicide and attempted suicide' (WHO 1991: 23).

Similarly, the *Health of the Nation* strategy for England aims both to reduce overall suicide rates, including those among people with a serious mental illness, and to improve the health and social functioning of people diagnosed mentally ill (Department of Health (1993a). Although mental illness was not originally designated a priority area in Scotland, more recently emphasis has also been placed on the prevention of illness and on the quality of life of people diagnosed mentally ill by the NHS in Scotland Management Executive (Scottish Office 1995).

Clearly, then, there is some considerable overlap between the aims of community care and those of health promotion, in that both policies identify the quality of life of people diagnosed mentally ill as a priority. The public fears which threaten to jeopardise community care therefore also pose a threat to health promotion goals. In addition, there is evidence to suggest that stigmatisation by local communities directly affects mental health service users. For example, in a study of long-term psychiatric patients living in community-based accommodation, Forrest (1992) found that these people felt far from integrated into their community. On the contrary, their attitudes to community care were largely negative as a result of their experience of ridicule and exclusion.

Where prevention is concerned there is also evidence that fear of stigmatisation may prevent people from seeking help with mental health problems before these become more serious. In a national survey carried out for the Defeat Depression Campaign organised jointly by the Royal Colleges of Psychiatrists and General Practitioners, 64 per cent of respondents agreed that people would be embarrassed to consult their GP for depression (Royal College of Psychiatrists 1995). Given that the prevalence of depression is now known to be much higher than previously estimated from general practitioners' records (Melzer *et al.* 1994), this would suggest that many people do indeed avoid seeking help with depression. In turn, this may undermine attempts to reduce suicide rates, since the incidence of suicide has been shown to be associated with depression (Wilkinson 1994). Under these circumstances, the possibility that media images of mental illness may contribute to stigmatisation clearly gives cause for concern.

The implications for journalists and broadcasters

On the basis of the discussion so far it might be supposed that the perspectives of those involved in implementing public policy would be in direct opposition to the views of journalists and broadcasters. While the former might be assumed to be concerned with defending the interests of people diagnosed mentally ill against negative media coverage, the latter might be supposed to be interested in producing a saleable product or, less cynically, in simply reflecting the views of society. However, for journalists and broadcasters themselves fair and accurate reporting is an issue of central concern, particularly in the light of recent threats to regulate the media and restrict their freedom through new legislation.

That this is the case is demonstrated by the codes of practice drawn up by the media's own professional organisations and regulatory bodies. For example, both the Chartered Institute of Journalists and the National Union of Journalists proscribe inaccurate or distorted reporting and the expression of conjecture or comment as fact, as does the code drawn up by the Guild of Editors, by which the UK magazine and newspaper industry has agreed to be bound. In addition, clause 15 of the Guild of Editors' code states explicitly that the press should avoid prejudicial or pejorative reference to any physical or mental illness.

Similarly, the Broadcasting Standards Council has recently revised their code of practice. In this second edition, concerns about the portrayal of mental illness are reflected in a new section on violence and mental health: 'Because some forms of human behaviour seem incomprehensible, the assumption may be made that the persons concerned are mentally ill. It is important in reporting some acts of criminal violence not to associate them uncritically with questions about the mental health of their perpetrators' (Broadcasting Standards Council 1994: 23–24).

The question of how mental illness is portrayed in the media is of interest, then, not only to mental health professionals and others involved in implementing public policy, but also to those who work in the media. To date, however, fears that media coverage and impact are largely negative have been founded on impressions formed from isolated reports and small-scale case studies. The collation of more substantial evidence through systematic research is therefore of crucial importance. In the following section we present a critical review of previous research.

Research review: the media and mental illness

A review of previous research into public beliefs about mental illness, and the part played by the media in shaping these, reveals that to date very little is known about either issue. Here we examine two bodies of relevant research: studies of beliefs and attitudes among the public in Britain and research into the impact of media images and their impact on beliefs and attitudes.

Beliefs and attitudes about mental illness

In Britain, only five studies of any significance have addressed the question of public beliefs and attitudes about mental illness. The five studies span the past 30 years, the earliest being undertaken by MacLean (1969) in the mid-1960s. Two of the five studies are national surveys (MORI 1979, Department of Health 1993b), while three focus on attitudes within particular cities or towns. These include MacLean's study, undertaken in Edinburgh, a survey of attitudes in two Worcestershire towns reported by Brockington *et al*. (1993) and by Hall *et al*. (1993), and a study undertaken in the north of England by Huxley (1993). The two national surveys and the Worcestershire study were relatively large scale in that they each involved close to 2,000 respondents. MacLean's study involved a sample of 500 people, while Huxley's was smaller in scale, involving 154 respondents.

Although small in number, the studies are not easy to review because differences in their design make it difficult to compare their findings. In the first place, they do not all share the same purpose. While two were designed as straightforward attempts to examine beliefs and attitudes (Department of Health, MacLean), the other three had rather different aims which are reflected in the issues they examine. The MORI survey was commissioned by MIND and the Mental Health Foundation to examine issues of relevance to employers and others who might make charitable donations to mental health causes. In contrast, the studies undertaken by Brockington and his colleagues and by Huxley shared the aim of assessing the impact of community care by comparing beliefs and attitudes in areas where community-based mental health services have been developed with those in other areas.

In addition to these divergent aims, the studies are based on research instruments which have as many differences as similarities. For example, MacLean, the Department of Health and Brockington *et al*. all used statements with which respondents are asked to indicate the extent of their agreement or disagreement. However, while MacLean developed her own statements in the course of two pilot studies, the Department of Health and Brockington *et al*. derived theirs from a North American instrument, the Community Attitudes to Mental Illness (CAMI) inventory. Similarly, although Hall *et al*. and Huxley used case vignettes in combination with fixed response or open questions, for the Worcestershire study Hall *et al*. adapted vignettes developed in North America, while Huxley constructed his own. The vignette approach consists of the investigator giving the respondent a written description of behaviour associated with a particular mental illness. The respondent is then asked questions about the person whose behaviour has been described. In contrast with these approaches, the MORI survey was based largely on a straightforward structured questionnaire, with one or two open questions.

Given their disparate aims and design, there seems little point in attempting to list or collate all the findings of these five studies. Instead, we examine the main themes which emerge in relation to three issues of particular concern: respondents' views about the causes of mental illness and appropriate sources of treatment; the extent to which respondents express sympathy or fear for people diagnosed mentally ill; and the extent to which they are willing to accept people diagnosed mentally ill as full members of society. On the basis of this review, we highlight a number of limitations concerning the methods used, before turning to examine what is known about media content and its influence on people's beliefs.

Beliefs about the causes and treatment of mental illness are important in that they can reveal underlying attitudes to people who are diagnosed mentally ill. For example, if mental illness is attributed to moral or other personal failings, this may well suggest an unsympathetic attitude. Similarly, if admission to hospital is regarded as an appropriate response, this might be indicative of a reluctance to accept people diagnosed mentally ill within local communities.

As far as causes are concerned, the research reviewed here suggests that the public are relatively sympathetic, in that social and environmental causes consistently emerge as more significant, in the opinion of respondents, than either personal failings or physiological factors. For example, MacLean reports that over 80 per cent of her respondents agreed with statements suggesting job worries, overwork and the stress of present-day living as the most likely causes. Similarly, the great majority of responses to an open question about causes asked by both MORI and Huxley revolved around general stress or specific problems relating to the family, money and work.

In contrast, less than half of MacLean's respondents agreed with statements suggesting lack of moral strength and physiological factors as causes, and this contrast was more marked in the later studies. Only 17 per cent of the MORI sample spontaneously mentioned physiological factors as a possible cause, with even fewer (4 per cent) mentioning weakness of character. In response to the same question, none of Huxley's respondents mentioned either, while only 16 per cent of the Department of Health sample agreed that 'lack of discipline or will power' was a main cause of mental illness.

The approach taken by the Worcestershire study to eliciting views about causes was rather different. For this study, respondents were shown case vignettes depicting four types of illness: paranoid schizophrenia, 'schizophrenic defect state', depression and obsessive neurosis. For each vignette they were asked to select the most likely causes of the behaviour described from a given list which included 'mental illness' alongside a range of social, environmental and physiological factors. Hall *et al.* report that mental illness was the most frequently selected cause only for the vignettes depicting paranoid schizophrenia and the 'defect state'. Even for these vignettes, it was selected by only 26 per cent and 18 per cent, respectively. As in the other four studies, social and environmental factors were selected more frequently than physiological factors for all four vignettes.

Responses to questions about appropriate sources of treatment suggest that a greater willingness to accept people diagnosed mentally ill within local communities has developed in the course of the three decades separating MacLean's study from the more recent research. While 94 per cent of MacLean's respondents agreed with a statement suggesting that people should be admitted to hospital as soon as they show signs of disturbance, only 21 per cent of the Department of Health respondents did so. Although differences in the wording of the statements presented may have had an effect, 81 per cent of respondents to the Department of Health survey also agreed that 'the best therapy. for many people with mental illness is to be part of a normal community', while 77 per cent agreed that 'as far as possible, mental health services should be provided through community based facilities'. However, only 41 per cent agreed that 'mental hospitals are an outdated means of treatment for people with mental illness', suggesting that attitudes are more complex than might appear to be the case from responses to other statements.

Again, the questions asked by Huxley and Hall *et al.* in relation to sources of treatment were rather different from those asked by other researchers. Whereas Huxley asked an open question about whether his respondents thought the people described in his vignettes needed help, and if so from whom, Hall *et al.* presented a list of possible sources of help from which respondents were asked to select the most appropriate. The responses obtained are not dissimilar, however, in that significant numbers of respondents to both studies did not appear to see medical sources of help as the most appropriate. In the case of Huxley's study, medical sources of help were mentioned by 55 per cent of respondents for a vignette depicting schizophrenia and by 31 per cent for post-natal depression.

This emphasis on non-medical sources of help was more striking among respondents to the Worcestershire study. Over all four vignettes, a friend was most frequently selected as the appropriate source of help (by 74 per cent of respondents), followed by a psychiatrist, general practitioner, social worker and neighbour, in that order. A psychiatrist was most frequently selected only for the paranoid schizophrenia vignette, and then by only just over half of respondents. A GP was the second most frequent choice for the obsessive neurosis vignette, joint second with a psychiatrist for the depression vignette, and third most frequent for the two schizophrenia vignettes. The other medical sources listed, a hospital doctor and a nurse, were among the least frequently chosen, ahead only of the police.

Overall, then, it appears that mental illness is seen as originating in social causes and that friends or other social supports are regarded as more appropriate than medicalised forms of treatment.

The view that these findings are indicative of sympathetic attitudes to people diagnosed mentally ill appears to be supported by further findings from three of the studies which used more direct measures of respondents' sympathy. Thus the Department of Health report substantial agreement (over 85 per cent) with statements such as 'people with mental illness have for far too long been the subject of ridicule' and 'we have a responsibility to provide the best care for the mentally ill'. Disagreement with statements suggesting a lack of sympathy, such as 'people with a mental illness don't deserve our sympathy' and 'increased spending on mental health services is a waste of money', was correspondingly high. Equally, Brockington *et al.* report that less than

2 per cent of respondents to the Worcestershire study had negative scores on a factor encompassing similar statements, while MacLean simply notes that the overwhelming majority of her respondents agreed with two statements directly expressing sympathy.

Alongside these expressions of sympathy, the majority of respondents to the three studies indicated that they did not regard people diagnosed mentally ill as dangerous. However, significant minorities did express a degree of fear in relation to some of the statements presented. Although 51 per cent of MacLean's sample disagreed with a statement suggesting simply that 'the mentally ill are dangerous', 33 per cent agreed. Not dissimilarly, although 66 per cent of respondents to the Department of Health survey agreed that 'people with a mental illness are less of a danger than most people suppose', opinion as to whether 'less emphasis should be placed on protecting the public from people with mental illness' was more evenly divided, with 38 per cent agreeing and 31 per cent disagreeing.

Some degree of ambivalence also emerges in relation to the extent to which people diagnosed mentally ill are accepted as full members of society, although attitudes again appear to have become more sympathetic over the past two decades as far as employment is concerned. Thus 39 per cent of MacLean's respondents were reluctant to accept that people who had experienced mental illness could hold responsible jobs, while only 18 per cent of respondents to the Department of Health survey expressed this view.

Although the Worcestershire study included a similar question about employment, the researchers incorporate responses to this with responses to other statements describing more personal social roles to produce a 'social restrictiveness' factor. In terms of this factor, they found that socially restrictive attitudes were generally rejected, but that 34 per cent of respondents did have negative scores. Had their analysis allowed for separate examination of scores on the different statements included, it may be that a trend suggested by MacLean's study and by the Department of Health survey would have been discernible. In both studies, respondents were increasingly less willing to accept people with experience of mental illness as closer social roles were suggested.

The same trend is in fact evident in the findings of the vignette-based section of the Worcestershire study reported by Hall *et al*. Here respondents were asked to indicate their willingness to engage in a range of social interactions with the four people described in the vignettes. The interactions were chosen to represent increasing social closeness, and on all four vignettes a clear increase in reluctance emerged as greater closeness was suggested. This was most sharply delineated for the paranoid schizophrenia vignette, but it was also marked for the other three.

Although neither the MORI survey nor Huxley's study directly examined respondents' acceptance of people diagnosed mentally ill, they did include questions about whether mental illness was perceived to be a source of embarrassment. Again, the results suggest some degree of ambivalence. In both studies, the majority of respondents agreed with a statement suggesting 'most people are embarrassed by mentally ill people'. However, when presented with a statement suggesting 'I am embarrassed by mentally ill people', only 27 per cent of respondents to the MORI survey and 31 per cent of Huxley's agreed.

While the findings outlined above therefore suggest some clear trends as far as sympathetic attitudes are concerned, there appears to be a degree of dissonance between the expression of sympathy and the extent to which people diagnosed mentally ill are accepted as full members of society. One of the main criticisms which can be made of the five studies is that their design precluded exploration of such potentially interesting findings. From a methodological perspective, however, their design also raises more specific problems which cast doubt on the validity even of those findings where a clearer trend appears to emerge.

Considering first the agree/disagree statements used by MacLean, the Department of Health and Brockington *et al.*, one problem is that these ignore the meanings attributed by respondents to the concepts being addressed. A striking example is the way in which questions are asked about 'mental illness' without any attempt to ascertain how respondents understand that concept. As a result, their views may well have been based on a quite different understanding of the issues being discussed. Certainly, responses to questions about causes and treatment suggest that the medical model is not widely shared by lay people, but the question of how respondents *do* understand mental illness remains largely unexplored, and the meaning of their views about causes and other issues therefore remains unknown.

A second problem concerns those studies which relied largely on pre-coded questions, whether alone or in conjunction with agree/disagree statements. In the first place, closed formats of this sort fail to recognise that our beliefs and attitudes are not fixed entities held in isolation from the social contexts in which we express them. Rather, as the work of discourse analysts has demonstrated, we construct our attitudes as we express them in the course of social interactions such as a research interview. When more open forms of questioning are used, variations in the attitudes expressed emerge more commonly than not, and the task of the researcher is therefore to understand how these make sense, rather than to make judgements about the truth or otherwise of particular statements (Potter and Wetherell 1987).

In addition, closed formats appear to encourage respondents to express positive attitudes (Brockman *et al.* 1979). As Brockington and his colleagues acknowledge, the presence of an interviewer may discourage respondents from selecting negative options from among those presented, particularly in the case of better educated respondents who may be more aware of professionally approved views. Although interviewers can be trained to minimise this 'halo' effect, the wording of the questions asked can also exert considerable pressure, and this certainly seems likely to be true as far as some of the Likert-type statements used in the research reviewed here are concerned. The most glaring examples are provided by statements intended to assess levels of sympathy such as 'people with mental illness have for far too long been the subject of ridicule', in which the ring of moral rhetoric would surely discourage dissent. Of the researchers concerned, only MacLean acknowledges this effect, and she is quite open about the value of her findings with respect to the expression of sympathetic attitudes: 'Both questions were a straightforward invitation to benevolence and it was scarcely to be expected that many people would express outright disagreement' (p. 48).

Finally, it cannot in any case be assumed that the positive sentiments expressed by most respondents in relation to these and other questions would be translated into action. This is particularly pertinent where care in the community is concerned. For example, even though respondents may well agree that 'residents have nothing to fear from people coming into their neighbourhood to obtain mental health services', as the Department of Health and Brockington *et al.* report, this would not necessarily be translated into benevolence towards people moving from a psychiatric hospital into their own neighbourhood. Equally, the widespread disagreement with the statement that 'increased spending on mental health services is a waste of money' reported by the same researchers can hardly be assumed to mean that respondents would be willing to pay higher taxes in order to improve services.

In view of these methodological weaknesses, the conclusion drawn by Brockman *et al.* about attitude measures of this type seems apposite: '... attitudes to the mentally ill are multi-faceted, highly complex and difficult to evaluate. To better understand them there is a need for full awareness of the biases and consequences of methodological factors. Even then, it is likely that the "handful"of social distance items used ... is inadequate to tap all the dimensions of such feelings' (p. 673).

Whether the findings generated by vignettes such as those used by Huxley and by Hall *et al.* are less suspect, as Brockman *et al.* go on to suggest, is debatable. Advocates of this approach propose that its strength lies in the provision of a context for the questions asked, so that assumptions about respondents' understanding of the abstract concept 'mental illness' are avoided. However, the context provided is based on the classification of behaviour into discrete 'illnesses', an approach which arguably only makes explicit the medical model implicit in other approaches, and which still leaves respondents' own understanding unexplored. In addition, as Hall *et al.* acknowledge, vignettes cannot take account of the effect on people's responses of characteristics such as the age and sex of the people described, and these are only two of an infinite number of factors which together make up the social context within which we make sense of and respond to the behaviour of other people. Moreover, when used in conjunction with pre-coded questions, as in the Worcestershire study, vignettes share some of the other weaknesses of attitude measures. Here too, beliefs and attitudes are assumed to be fixed entities, and the likelihood of producing a 'halo' effect is not reduced.

In summary, then, these methodological weaknesses mean that the information available from previous research into beliefs about mental illness is very limited. For our own study, we were concerned to use methods which would enable us to explore how beliefs are shaped within particular social contexts and thus contribute to the development of knowledge in an area not addressed by previous research.

Media content and its impact on beliefs and attitudes

As noted earlier, there is also a dearth of information about media coverage of mental illness and its impact on public beliefs. Only three studies have examined media content in relation to mental health issues in any depth and of these, two were undertaken in North America. A further six studies have attempted to assess the impact of media images, both negative and positive, on beliefs and attitudes, but these have been too limited in their scope and methods to shed much light on the matter.

The first of the three studies examining media content was undertaken by Day and Page (1986) in Canada. The researchers rated 103 newspaper reports concerning people described as mentally ill for tone and ideology. The representations which emerged were then compared with the Canadian psychiatric hospital admission statistics for 1984. On the basis of their analysis, Day and Page conclude that mental illness was misrepresented in the reports. For example, schizophrenia was overrepresented, being cited as a diagnosis in 77 per cent of cases compared with a hospital admission rate of 37 per cent. In addition, the images of mental illness conveyed by the reports were characterised by negative stereotypes and assumptions, resulting in an implicit portrayal of a homogenous, parasitic group with no positive social identity. Dangerousness, unpredictability, dependency and transience were among the main characteristics portrayed.

On the basis of a second study, this time of television coverage in the United States, Signorielli (1989) draws some similar conclusions. For the purposes of the study, week-long samples of prime time, networked drama were collected annually over a period of 16 years. An analysis of these programmes revealed that characters portrayed as mentally ill were more likely to be depicted both as violent and as victims than any other type of character. They were also more likely to be portrayed as 'bad' and least likely to be portrayed as 'good'. In addition, as the dramatic plots unfolded almost half of the mentally ill characters were depicted as failures, compared to fewer than a fifth of all characters, and this impression of failure was closely associated with their inability to obtain or hold down a job.

In the North American context, then, there is some evidence to suggest that media representations of mental illness are largely negative, and that violence, victimisation and failure are predominant themes. However, although there is undoubtedly a degree of overlap between North American and British television drama, it seems unlikely that many of the news stories analysed by Day and Page were reported in Britain, and the extent to which these findings are generalisable to the British context is therefore questionable. The only study undertaken in this area in Britain sheds little light on this issue, largely because of significant differences in the methods employed.

For this study, Wober (1991) drew on information collected from a nationally representative panel of television viewers to examine perceptions of the extent and quality of coverage of mental illness. Over 2,000 respondents answered questions about these issues which were included in a diary accounting for their appreciation of programmes during the week ending 20 January 1991. On the basis of their responses, Wober reports that documentaries, one-off plays and dramas were seen as the sort of programmes which dealt both most extensively and most sympathetically with mental illness. Situation comedies were considered to portray mental illness only rarely and when they did so a quarter of respondents found them particularly unsympathetic. Similarly, the veracity of coverage was considered to be high in documentaries, news programmes and plays, but low in situation comedies and adventure action features. Soap operas were rated average to low in terms of both the extent of coverage and its quality. Wober concludes from these findings that British television portrayals of mental illness are largely positive.

Although genuine differences between North American and British television coverage might account for the marked discrepancy between Wober's conclusion and Signorielli's in the United States, this might equally well be a methodological artifact. In the first place, while the North American study was restricted to prime time drama, Wober examined a wider range of programming. As has been seen, British viewers rated soap operas and adventure action features less positively than other types of programme. Had the study been restricted to this kind of drama, it is therefore likely that the findings would have been closer to Signorielli's. In addition, the criteria used by both researchers to assess the quality of coverage are open to interpretation, a problem neither study addresses. For example, while Signorielli clearly regards portrayals of victimisation as negative, respondents to the British survey might have described such portrayals as 'sympathetic' on the grounds that they evoked their own sympathy. Similarly, portrayals of mentally ill people as 'failures', which Signorielli regards as negative, might have been seen by respondents to the British survey as 'true to life', and therefore counted by Wober as positive. Finally, in drawing his conclusion Wober does not take into account the relative impact of different programme genres on the viewing audience. It is arguable, for example, that programmes like soap operas and adventure action features which attract large audiences and evoke an emotional response are likely to have a greater impact on beliefs and attitudes than 'drier' programmes like documentaries which attract smaller audiences.

None of the three studies reviewed above were designed to assess the impact of media coverage on beliefs and attitudes. As was seen earlier, however, six further studies have attempted to examine this issue. Of these studies, four were intended to assess the impact of coverage deemed negative by the researchers. All four studies relied on measures similar to those which have been employed to examine public beliefs and attitudes in Britain, and they therefore share the methodological weaknesses of the research reviewed earlier. In addition, each study has internal methodological flaws which cast further doubt on the validity of the findings.

The first of the four studies, undertaken in the United States by Steadman and Cocozza (1977), aimed to examine public perceptions of 'the criminally insane' and to explore how these perceptions might be related to media coverage. A random sample of 413 householders took part in the study. They were asked to indicate the extent to which a series of statements applied to 'most people', 'mental patients' and 'the criminally insane'. In addition, they were asked whether they could recall news coverage concerning someone who was criminally insane. Two main findings emerged. First, the underlying concepts which were used to distinguish 'mental patients' from 'most people' were dangerousness and unpredictability. Where 'the criminally insane' were concerned, these concepts merged so that unpredictability became part of people's conceptualisation of the danger posed. Second, the great majority of those identified as criminally insane on the basis of media reports were mass murderers or assassins of presidents and other public figures.

Steadman and Cocozza point out that from a legal perspective these perceptions of criminal insanity are inaccurate. For example, the vast majority of people who are legally defined as criminally insane have committed crimes against property or minor offences while only 14 per cent had ever been accused of murder, let alone convicted, at the time the research was undertaken. As the researchers acknowledge, however, the connection they were able to make between their respondents' misperceptions and media coverage was only tentative, and it is possible that other factors played some part. The same caveat applies to two further North American studies undertaken by Domino (1983) and Wahl and Lefkowits (1989).

Domino's research aimed to examine the impact of the film *One Flew Over the Cuckoo's Nest* on college students. Prior to the release of the film, he administered a questionnaire designed to assess attitudes among a sample of 146 students. The questionnaire was then re-administered three months after the release of the film to 124 of the students, 85 of whom had seen it and 39 of whom had not. Domino reports that there was no significant difference in attitudes prior to the release of the film between those students who later saw it and those who did not. After the release of the film, however, the attitudes of the students who had seen it were significantly less positive than the attitudes of those who had not.

Domino concludes on the basis of his findings that the film had a negative impact. However, weaknesses in the research design mean this conclusion is open to question. In particular, the students were not randomly allocated to different groups but chose for themselves in the ordinary course of their social lives whether or not to see the film. For this reason it is by no means certain that the change in attitudes Domino reports among those who saw it was in fact due to the film itself. It is not unlikely, for example, that the students who saw the film were more regular cinemagoers than those who did not. If this were true, then they might have been exposed to more films in the three months before completing the second questionnaire than the other students, and it could be that this wider exposure had influenced their attitudes rather than *One Flew Over the Cuckoo's Nest* alone. Equally, variables other than frequency of going to the cinema which Domino neither examined nor controlled for may have had some influence on their attitudes.

The aim of the study undertaken by Wahl and Lefkowits (1989) was to examine the impact of a television film based on a real incident involving a man who was committed to a mental hospital and who murdered his wife while on a day pass. To achieve this, they showed the film to 86 psychology students. At the same time a control group of 19 students watched a different film featuring murder but not mental illness. Immediately after seeing the films the students were asked to complete a standardised questionnaire based on the CAMI inventory.

Wahl and Lefkowits report a significant association between the films seen by the students and their expressed attitudes. Those who watched the film featuring mental illness as well as murder saw a greater need for hospitalisation and expressed more negative views about community care than the other students. They also expressed less sympathy for people suffering from mental illness, and more concern about their potential dangerousness. As the researchers acknowledge, however, they did not assess the students' attitudes prior to seeing the two films. As a result, it remains uncertain whether the attitudes of the students who saw the target film changed or whether they were different from those of the other students to begin with. In addition, other variables such as age and gender which may have influenced the findings were not examined or controlled for. Finally, because the students' attitudes were assessed only immediately after watching the films, it is possible that the findings reflect a momentary response to the target film which would have dissipated over time.

Support for this final point emerges from the only British study to address the impact of negative media coverage. Undertaken by Appleby and Wessely (1988), this study examines responses to reporting of the Hungerford massacre, during which Michael Ryan killed 15 people before committing suicide. Some three months prior to the massacre, the researchers had carried out a survey of public attitudes to people suffering from mental illness. A quota sample of 965 people were asked to indicate the extent to which they agreed or disagreed with three statements: 'mentally ill people are likely to be violent'; 'people who commit horrific crimes are likely to be mentally ill'; and 'people suffering from mental illness should be encouraged to live in the community'. While fewer respondents agreed with the first statement than disagreed, responses to the second question were more equally divided, with 47 per cent agreeing and 43 per cent disagreeing. Despite this, 57 per cent agreed that mentally ill people should be encouraged to live in the community, while only 21 per cent disagreed.

Two weeks after the massacre, the researchers repeated the survey with a further quota sample of 998 people. On this occasion there was little difference in responses to the first and third statements, but agreement with the second statement about the link between mental illness and the perpetrators of horrific crimes increased significantly to 54 per cent. Although they acknowledge that the part played by media coverage in this apparent shift in attitudes cannot be demonstrated conclusively, Appleby and Wessely suggest that it almost certainly played a large part. However, on repeating their survey for a third time some six months after the massacre the researchers found no significant differences between responses to any of the statements and those obtained prior to the massacre.

Although this study therefore supports the view that the impact of media coverage may be short-lived, Appleby and Wessely concur with the other researchers whose work has been reviewed so far in suggesting that efforts should be made to encourage more positive media coverage. However, the question of whether such coverage would have a correspondingly positive influence on public attitudes has been addressed by only two studies, both undertaken in Britain on behalf of broadcasting organisations.

The first of the two studies, undertaken for the BBC by Belson (1967), examined the impact of a documentary series about mental health issues on viewers' attitudes. A sample of people who had seen at least one of the programmes and a further sample of people who had not were invited to attend a meeting where they completed a series of tests. A total of 800 people attended. After controlling for pre-existing differences between the two groups, Belson reports that the people who had watched the programmes were somewhat more knowledgeable about mental illness and rather more confident about the effectiveness of treatment. They also expressed greater willingness to associate with former or current patients in some respects, though not in relation to offering them employment. In addition, they were slightly less likely to feel that mental illness was 'something to keep quiet about' and expressed more feelings of sympathy for people diagnosed mentally ill. Although some of these differences were slight, Belson concludes that the series had a positive impact.

The second study which attempted to examine the impact of more positive coverage was undertaken by Wober (1989) for the Independent Broadcasting Authority. Like the research described earlier, this study drew on information obtained from an audience appreciation survey. During October and November 1986, Channel 4 had broadcast 12 programmes about mental health issues which were intended to be educational and informative. At the end of the year questions designed to address the impact of the series were included in the audience survey. On the basis of responses to these questions Wober reports that viewing of the programmes was associated with a greater willingness to associate with someone who had been in psychiatric hospital, but not with other attitudes towards people suffering from mental illness. As Wober acknowledges, these findings do not prove a programme viewing effect, because no information was available about respondents' attitudes prior to the Channel 4 campaign. Nevertheless, he concludes that the campaign probably did have a positive impact.

While the findings reported by Belson and Wober therefore appear to suggest that positive coverage can have a beneficial, if limited, impact, both studies again relied on standardised attitude measures. Just as these measures are unable to take into account the part played by social contexts in the construction of beliefs and attitudes, so they are unable to account for the complexities of the way in which we interpret media messages. As other researchers have demonstrated, for example, we may reject or negotiate media messages by citing contradictions within media accounts, or through reference to our own experiences and those of others (Philo 1990, Miller *et al.* 1992; Kitzinger 1993).

In the light of this previous research, we were concerned that our own study should achieve two aims. First, we wanted to provide a systematic analysis of the way in which the British mass media portray mental health issues, since research of this type has not previously been undertaken. Second, we were concerned to develop research methods which would allow us to explore the complex processes involved in the interpretation of media messages.

CHAPTER 2

Selling suffering: mental illness and media values

Lesley Henderson

Introduction

Negative images of mental health and illness pervade our media, yet it is too simplistic to assume that this is due merely to badly informed or unsympathetic programme-makers. This chapter examines some of the factors which influence media accounts of mental illness and offers an analysis of why, from a range of available representations, we see a very limited and distorted view of people with mental illness. It is crucial to do this for two reasons. First, it is important to contextualise media portrayals of mental illness across a range of media formats: 'the media' is itself an unhelpful term which suggests a single entity with a homo-geneous approach to this area. It is essential that we differentiate between media outlets and approaches to the subject matter. Second, if 'alternative' voices are to intervene in the kinds of images which exist in this area or create their own, more positive representations, campaign-ing groups must understand the media values which underpin such portrayals. In short, the workings of the media must first be understood if they are to be changed.

The central argument here is that television accounts of mental illness are the products of a series of negotiations involving production personnel. Underpinning the decision-making process is the constant pressure for audience ratings. This concern can override any social responsibility to present more balanced or accurate representations of mental ill health and can undermine the possibilities for images which convey more challenging messages about the subject.

This chapter analyses the production processes which condition tele-vision images of mental health, focusing on 'non-news' programming. The sample includes 15 interviews with a range of production per-sonnel over a two-year period, 1993 to 1995. The sample is structured to include production workers throughout the broadcast hierarchy and across different media formats. I therefore interviewed executive pro-ducers, producers, story-editors, script-editors and writers who work in factual and fictional television programming. For example, production teams for each of the major soap operas/drama series were contacted: *Coronation Street* (ITV); *EastEnders* (BBC); *Brookside* (Channel 4) and *Casualty* (BBC). I also spoke with the producer of *Takin' Over the Asylum* (BBC), a comedy/drama series which had a distinctive approach to the subject of mental health. Finally, in terms of factual programming, I interviewed documentary producers who worked both independently and 'in-house' for the BBC and who had extensive experiences of making films in the mental health field.

The negotiating process

Crucial to understanding 'how the media works' is the recognition that what we ultimately see on our television screens is the outcome of a complex *negotiation* process. Writers, journalists and programme-makers are not autonomous. All must work under a series of competing pressures. Every representation of mental illness is therefore, a product based on input from a number of individuals throughout the broadcast hierarchy. Personal and organisational agendas may conflict in the decision-making process and constraints of economics, hierarchy and genre inter-connect to shape media representations. However, the key factor which underpins all of these concerns is the need to attract and maintain audiences.

This section looks at how perceptions of audience needs can affect the selection of media items and how they are presented.

Education versus entertainment

A frequent criticism levelled at media images of mental illness is that the portrayal is 'unrealistic'. This might be due to the rarity of the condition which is being portrayed or how 'true to life' the actions of the protagonist are. Campaigners urge media workers to 'check their facts' but, in practice, the emphasis upon background research differs substantially from programme to programme. The main problem appears to be that 'research' is often regarded as the remit solely of documentaries or 'hard' news programming. Many of those involved in producing television entertainment perceive 'research' as a necessary burden which may hinder the 'pure' process of making watchable TV drama. To stick too rigidly to 'facts and figures' also brings the ethos of the programme dangerously close, in their eyes, to 'public education'. The fear is that audiences may 'switch off' if they believe that the entertainment genre is 'lecturing' rather than 'entertaining' them. Few writers or producers would deny that mental health is a subject that requires sensitivity and caution yet it is apparent that difficult topics of this kind provoke a double dilemma for them. This dilemma can be termed 'entertainment versus education'. Here, for example, the producer of *Coronation Street* outlines the programmes' remit:

The interesting thing about 'The Street' is that people feel comfortable with it and people can watch it as a family. All our stories are generated by the characters in the programme. We are not issue-led. We don't sit around and say 'Let's have a story about rape' ... Many people write to us and say 'Would you debate this issue? And would you please let everyone know it is National Breast Feeding Week?' and I have to write back and say 'No' to everybody because we then just become a political machine. It would become propaganda that we were churning out and we are supposed to be entertaining people, not brainwashing them.

The Channel 4 soap opera *Brookside* selects potential storylines by a radically different method. Rather than being character-led, the programme is explicitly 'issue-led' and has dealt consistently with challenging storylines such as HIV/AIDS and 'date rape'. Although writers may propose ideas in meetings, it is not unusual for storyline developments to come directly from 'the top'. The executive producer and producer of the show have bi-annual meetings where the long-term strategy for the show is mapped out: statistical trends of unemployment, crime and social problems are used to compose 'demographically correct' plots. The producer argues that *Brookside* can offer a far more 'realistic' portrayal of social issues than other dramas. As he comments, 'If someone has a breakdown in *Brookside* they never get over it because life's not like that.' However, this focus on social realism is balanced constantly with the perceived needs of audiences. Storylines therefore might arise from a well-researched base but for audience enjoyment they must then be 'packaged': As the producer explains:

The trick is to take all [the statistics] and not do a documentary on it which you know people will just go 'It's just facts and figures, it's a documentary'. The trick is to package it in a story which has become soap opera because you make it entertainment then. You make people guess and use all the tricks of soap opera which is 'Will she do this? Will she do that?'

Despite an initially socially realistic approach to subject material, values of entertainment and acceptability to audiences are crucial. Programme-makers generally do not wish to be perceived by audiences as 'educating' them, particularly in the soap opera genre. This is seen to conflict with the role of that particular format. By 'packaging' stories for audience consumption, *Brookside* sees itself as provoking audience debate rather than providing audiences with clear social messages which can be mistaken for 'education'. As the producer argues: '[Audiences] are not finding in *Brookside* any answers. That's how you educate, you give people answers ... If I started to believe we are educating, God you know? What have I become? I couldn't!'

Writers and research

Attitudes towards research are also connected intrinsically to attitudes towards the writing process. For drama writers, research can be viewed as 'contaminating' the act of writing. Thus even if research material is available in the form of press cuttings, for example, many still prefer to rely upon the 'psychological truth' as they see it. As an experienced *Brookside* writer commented:

> I just like to [write] from my imagination and we do have a researcher on *Brookside* who picks up any factual or technical things you've got wrong. Even then sometimes they will come and tell you something which you would have to write down in about five pages and it's so boring you just forget it and go for the truth of the feelings.

This experience was common to writers across television drama series. For example, I spoke with a storyline consultant for BBC's *EastEnders* who worked on particularly sensitive items such as child sexual abuse and HIV / AIDS. He agreed that 'research' is important for potentially distressing subjects but prefers to write subjectively. In his words: 'what you get from that type of research is the official line and the official line is not always what happens'.

Constraints of narrative pace

An additional influence on television output stems from the belief that viewers require 'stories' with narrative pace. In the words of one experienced drama writer, 'we must keep telling stories or risk losing momentum' and, more importantly, audiences. For example, a soap will concentrate and condense storylines, balancing realistic timescales with viewing pleasures. *Brookside*'s producer justified this, saying: 'You have to remember that the audience are rather fickle and switch in and out of soaps. They also like pace or the audience starts to think "Oh is this still going on?" So even though the audience say they like reality, they sometimes don't.'

We show in Chapter 6 that this rapid turnover of storylines can have a very negative impact on those who experience periods of distress and who see fictional characters move swiftly from illness to health. A scriptwriter for *Brookside* justified the priorities of the soap opera by arguing that stories are simply: 'concentrated in a way that's not absolutely true to get the maximum drama out of them and to get the debate seriously going about what happens in real life'.

Narrative concerns are not confined to fictional programming. For documentary producers, the need for audience-pleasing pace and structure can affect decisions about the content of their films. As a BBC producer explains, this can be at the expense of a more balanced picture of mental illness. Here she recounts her experiences of filming in a psychiatric institution:

> There are two stages I think where what you need as a programme-maker conflicts with basically what is there – one is in the filming of it and another is in the editing. You are looking for some drama. You know you need a dramatic moment and you know you need it relatively soon and you know you need a resolution. There were times where we were absolutely frantic to get a section because we knew it was an aspect that was going to be covered.

Regardless of how frequently sections happen in the real world we knew it was going to work for television.

The required narrative pace is often at odds with the reality of mental ill health, where people may recover and then become ill again. In the view of some television personnel, their own perceptions of audience needs must be prioritised. One documentary producer recognised the potential for presenting misleading pictures of mental illness and 'exploiting' interviewees but then commented that: 'There is no point in making boring telly about boring people.' As she noted:

> In the editing what you need to make telly work is a story. No television programme or the sorts of documentaries we were making would have held without a story, perhaps without narrative development. Now that doesn't reflect reality. There were an awful lot of times where people were being fairly interestingly ill, then getting better then more ill again so what we did in the editing was to generate narrative.

Dramatising mental illness: two case studies

To illustrate how the production process works in practice, this section examines the factors which influenced two recent soap opera storylines. In our original content sample period (April 1993) both *Coronation Street* (ITV) and *Brookside* (C4) ran storylines which were found to have made a profound impact on audiences (See Philo *et al.* 1993).

In late 1991, the producer and executive producer of *Brookside* decided to introduce a storyline which would tackle domestic violence. Although the topic was potentially controversial it was also 'visually, very exciting – no other soap opera had done this before'. In March 1993, *Brookside* introduced the character of 'Trevor Jordache', who had been released from prison for violently assaulting his wife. *Brookside*'s producer denies that the programme intended to frame Trevor as mentally ill but our research found that audiences saw Trevor as a stereotypical 'psychopath' (see Chapter 4 and Henderson 1996). The production team argue that audiences were influenced by wider press coverage which dubbed the character 'Psycho Trevor'. As the producer stated here: 'We never said Trevor was mentally ill. It was the media itself putting on words like "Psycho Trevor". We'd set out to say we don't know what caused [his behaviour]; it might be mental illness. We don't know.'

Coronation Street ran a concurrent storyline where 'Carmel', a young Irish nanny, develops an erotic obsession with her employer's husband. She was clearly labelled throughout the story as 'mentally ill' and 'in need of a psychiatrist'. The Carmel story was described by a *Coronation Street* writer as '*The Hand that Rocks The Cradle* meets *Fatal Attraction*' – a reference to two popular feature films where family life is jeopardised by a 'disturbed' and potentially violent female. The story was generated in a writers' meeting by a member of the production team, as a script-writer describes:

There are about fourteen script-writers on the programme and what happens is we have a story conference every third Monday and basically we just float ideas around the room and then it is discussed from that point on and plotted through. We are actually four months ahead with storylines.

Background research

The *Brookside* research team gathered interview material with male per-petrators and female survivors of domestic violence for the writers to base Trevor's characterisation on. *Coronation Street* did not take any special advice on Carmel's condition. Her character was developed using a feature on 'erotomania' which they found in the American magazine *Vanity Fair*. As one writer told me:

We used that [article] and that would really explain to you about the whole psychology of Carmel. It is a brilliant article based on a couple of case studies in America. There were loads of court cases about it and a really long trial. The actual story did come before we heard about the article so that's not really what triggered [it] off, but as part of the research when we read that it really helped to bring the storyline together. In the conferences as well all the writers were discussing it.

Erotomania is an extraordinarily rare condition and in fact most of the details of Carmel's characterisation were inaccurate. For example, the object of affection is usually someone of high status and not known personally to the sufferer. The storyline did, however, conform to the classic soap opera ingredients of high suspense and drama. It terrified audiences who watched a 'disturbed' and manipulative woman threaten the security of a regular soap family. As the producer describes here:

Carmel, the nanny from hell and stories like that [are very strong]. Where you get someone new like Carmel who introduces a catalyst into a happy family and suddenly it all sort of festers and turns bad. I mean there's a really good story. I like those stories better than in the old days 'a train crashes into a viaduct'.

If the priority is audience ratings, concerns about the accuracy of the representation can be overridden – what matters is the quest for a 'good story'.

The importance of casting

Soap operas take risks when they introduce new characters. Audiences can take as long as one year to build loyalty and both *Coronation Street* and *Brookside* created new characters especially for these storylines. Production teams for both programmes identified 'casting the role' as of crucial importance. *Brookside* overcame potential problems with audi-ences by scripting Trevor for a 'light comedy' actor who was familiar to audiences from previous television roles. The producer outlines how audiences can determine their choice of actor and storyline development:

[Audiences] affect how you cast and how you write it because you know that if you portray the baddie, the perpetrator as from day one – the baddie – and have no sympathy at all for him then people will just not engage in the story. You have to play against [the fact that] you know the audience will fall into that trap of 'he looks like a baddie therefore he must be one'. So we purposely cast Bryan Murray because he was a likeable actor. So right from day one they would think, 'Oh I quite like him, he's a nice guy, doesn't he usually play the nice guy?' The minute people saw him on screen he had a history and we knew we had to drive this story fast.

A 'likeable actor' was chosen, therefore, to keep audiences guessing about future plot twists. In fact 'Trevor' is eventually murdered and the production wanted to build suspense in the audiences about his eventual fate. As one *Brookside* writer explained: 'If people just see a psychopath up on the screen then they say "Yeah, he deserves to die" as soon as he walks on screen.'

The casting of 'Carmel' was similarly important. *Coronation Street* therefore chose a 'fresh-faced' actress who could appear 'normal' to audiences and disguise her 'true character'. As a scriptwriter commented: 'It was very important in the casting to believe that she was this home-loving girl because if you did cast somebody who looked slightly dodgy then it immediately gave it away and I thought that [the actress] played it very well.'

Soap storylines rely upon maintaining audience tensions. The assumption is that an actor who 'looked' like someone who was mentally disturbed would deprive viewers of mounting suspense as their 'true' character unfolds over forthcoming episodes. Both characters were outsiders to the programme rather than regular personalities, so that audiences would not be faced with conflicts of sympathy. Perhaps to confirm this outsider status, 'Carmel' and 'Trevor' were both given Irish identities.

The panto syndrome

Soap operas use a series of conventions and codes to convey information to their audiences. The producer of *Coronation Street* described the 'Carmel' story as particularly 'strong' as it conformed to the classic technique where 'the audience knows more than the characters in the show do'. She described this as 'the panto syndrome'.

It's almost like 'He's behind you!'. That syndrome where the audience is saying 'You fool!' where you [the viewer] know that the author lets you into information where you see both characters' lives but they're not privy to that information

Brookside used similar devices to frame the narrative for audiences.

The team worked on a series of deliberate techniques designed to draw audiences into the fictional predicament. Much narrative suspense rested on whether or not Trevor had indeed changed his abusive behaviour. In a series of episodes he attempts to convince his wife,

Mandy, that he should be allowed to return to the family. A particularly successful technique was to end a scene with a lingering shot of Trevor's face after he has turned away from Mandy. The tension increases for audiences as Trevor's 'look' signals that he should not be trusted. *Brookside*'s producer explains why this works for audiences:

> You'd see him [Trevor] with his back to Mandy and you just see a look on his face, which she couldn't see and then you're setting up in the audience's mind 'Oh, this fella isn't straight' and that's great because that gives a lot of tension for the audience.

Ratings versus responsibility?

I have identified a series of decisions concerning 'Carmel' and 'Trevor' where audience pleasures were prioritised. However, production teams rarely admit that viewing pleasures can subordinate other concerns. Thus *Brookside*'s producer denies that potentially controversial story-lines are run specifically to increase ratings. He argues that there is simply 'no point' in producing challenging storylines unless audiences watch them: 'It wasn't about ratings. It was just the plain fact of "well we only do this so that people can watch". That's the point. There's no point in doing this and thinking "oh we've lost, no-one's watching it" so we knew we had to make them watch it.'

Coronation Street's producer also denies that the programme would include a storyline simply to attract audiences. She does, however, admit that there are pressures due to the long-term popularity of the programme with the additional pressures of commercial television. As she says here: 'If you are producing a show which regularly tops the ratings, the advertisers want to advertise in the breaks and the pressure is to be consistently good within the parameters.'

Soap operas attract large and diverse audiences and productions are aware of their power to communicate with audiences. In contrast with other drama series, *Coronation Street* is viewed as distinct in its use of this 'power'. *Coronation Street*'s producer believes that:

> *EastEnders* and *Brookside* have chosen to use that power to give a message to the British public. What we've done is chosen to use that power to entertain the British public. To give them good television. We aren't thrusting issues down their throat because they get enough of that with news and documentaries.

Documenting 'reality'

Production personnel who are involved in creating dramatic representations of mental illness are keen to draw a distinction between themselves and 'news media'. A familiar cry is 'we're not a documentary,' suggesting first that drama should be excused from the need for factual basis and secondly, that a format 'documentary' is inarguably more concerned with presenting 'the truth'. The genres are different but the problems with misrepresentation of people with mental illness are common to both. As a format the documentary may appear to be a more appropriate space for positive images of mental health. People with mental health problems can appear on screen telling their stories in their own words. However, the production process is more complex than may first appear. I will now look at some problems which are specific to the documentary form and examine in turn how the constraints of access, medical control, broadcast hierarchy, and assumptions about potential audiences affect the ways in which mental health is represented.

Groups who campaign for more accurate representations in the area of mental health view 'access to the media' as of acute importance. For example, organisations of users of services have begun to put themselves forward to speak on television and present their views. We discussed this with documentary producers and found that access to people with mental health problems is, for them, a key factor. A BBC producer outlined the problems she encountered in making a series of films with the patients of one community health team. In her view, although the filming process involved a series of compromises and negotiations it was still ultimately easier to record the experiences of people in psychiatric care than other groups of people in distress. For example, issues of privacy can be minimised by filming within a hospital environment rather than someone's home. Thus in choosing to portray this particular group, programme makers might overcome potential access problems but the resulting representation is very limited in the range of conditions and treatments which are included. As a producer acknowledges:

> ... the most controlled way to see someone who was mentally ill was in hospital. We could just be there. We weren't invading their privacy. We could just be there in the ward and we were there for weeks and months and ... they would see us around and we kind of became part of this very weird hospital environment but it completely skewed the sorts of people and the sort of ways we portrayed both mental illness and the way it was treated.

Producers must balance the needs of three groups: the production crew, the medical profession and the patients. Each group has competing needs and concerns which may actively work against the aims of the others. Key issues here are access and control. Before a production team can even approach someone in psychiatric care, they must first secure the agreement of the medical staff. Here the BBC producer outlines common problems:

> The most insidious [problem] is that mental health professionals protect to an unwarranted degree the privacy of their patients. They do that in the very honest belief ... that if the general public knew that this person had a mental health problem they would be treated less well, they would be shunned and they would be discriminated against. So an awful lot of people flatly said 'No, no I wouldn't feel happy allowing you anywhere near them' ... and there is such a medical hierarchy here that the medics by far have the greatest say and

a lot of them felt for the very best of motives [that the patients should not take part] but that took away from the individuals' right to decide what they wanted to do. The question wasn't even put to them.

Medical staff may use the fear of future stigmatisation to dissuade patients from identifying themselves in a television film. One producer, who interviewed patients who had been institutionalised for many years, described how medical staff will discourage patients from 'remembering what they have been taught to forget'. As this producer explains:

The medical profession have said [to the patients] 'I wouldn't be interviewed if I were you', 'It will get worse when you go out', 'you're going to be stigmatised when you go outside', that's a very common one or 'I wouldn't give an interview if I were you because you don't want to remember what happened to you do you? That's all past now, you're all right now'.

However, all of the producers I spoke with believed these medical concerns to be unfounded. In their view, audience reaction vindicated their decision to film such interviews. As an independent producer commented:

If you let someone who has been in an institution take the risk and say 'No, I do want to say why I was put into X institution' I know from the audience response, from people who ring the Channel or from people who write to me afterwards, that it is sympathetic to that person's point of view and it is less sympathetic to the medical system that put them there. So the stigma is transferred to the medical profession rather than the individual.

Another factor which influences 'who speaks' in a documentary of this type is the degree of 'control' which medical staff have over the hospital environment and the patients. This control can thus extend to the finished product as staff, rather than the crew, decide 'who is seen' and 'when'. One BBC producer saw this as having a profound effect on the series that she made:

In the mental health arena [the medical profession] are so used to control. They control the patients, they control the hospital environments and having a television crew there who aren't subject to your control – they are outside of it – is very threatening. So it wasn't always easy to talk to people just when you wanted to and if there hadn't been that degree of second-level control going on we would have made a completely different set of programmes.

Once permission is granted from the medical professionals there is the question of gaining patient's consent. Some producers I interviewed had experiences of filming very distressed people within psychiatric wards and there were clear ethical considerations. Particularly problematic was the fact that patients who were disturbed may not fully understand the implications of giving their consent. Medical staff too were acutely aware of their responsibilities as carers to protect the interests of their patients. For the same producer this issue was fraught with difficulties and severely jeopardised the level of 'control' which the production team retained over the completed programme:

> When people are extremely ill they are not able to make the decisions they would make when they are not ill, so it was very important that [the medical profession] had a way of controlling that but that put huge constraints on us as programme makers because the one thing that's very difficult is to give up editorial control because then it becomes a different piece. The only way we could get access to patients at all was to agree that they had the right to veto once they were well enough to do so.

This 'veto' removed power from the production crew to the medical staff who decided 'if' and 'when' their patients were 'fully *compos mentis*'. The veto also provided an obstacle to the content of the film which had intended to 'show very ill patients, as much as possible'.

The issue of gaining 'informed' consent is more complex than simply securing a signature on a legal document. Patients may experience 'blackouts' or simply not comprehend the full implications of giving permission. Patients may have literacy problems or be unable to understand the legal wording on forms. Techniques designed by producers to communicate the experience of being filmed included showing the interviewee on a TV monitor. One producer, however, saw the concept of 'informed consent' as ultimately impossible. As she says:

> I would always go to great lengths to explain to someone what we're going to do [but] I think there is a limit to how successful this business of asking permission is. What are you asking their permission to do? To cut their half hour interview down to 10 minutes? I think it's respecting their absolute right to say 'No, I don't want to be filmed' and in that sense it serves a function but it doesn't get across the nature of the media.

Self-selecting patients

Another factor, raised by producers, that influenced documentary accounts was that patients are 'self-selecting', which meant that the range of mental health problems was not represented. One producer believed that by this process of self-selection, the patients themselves contribute to the unbalanced picture which exists. She believed that if you are 'a chronic schizophrenic' or 'psychotic' then there is little to lose by identifying yourself on television:

> Patients were very self-selective and I think this affects the image that in documentary comes across about mental health because there are only certain sorts of people who feel able to stand up and say 'I have a mental illness and this is what it means for me and here I am'. The image of mental illness is very weighted towards the extreme end of mental illness [because] people who are seriously ill have very little to lose. We got a couple of personality disorders, some people with manic depression and they would say 'yes' to begin with but they had too much to lose by it and were too afraid of what their friends, neighbours, colleagues would say if they stood up and said 'I've got a mental illness' so the people who did it were almost professionally mentally ill people. The balance was definitely skewed.

Control from 'the people upstairs'

A crucial factor which influences media accounts across factual and fictional television is the level of control exerted by the broadcast hierarchy. Media workers are all subject to degrees of control 'from above' or, as one *Casualty* writer described it, 'the people upstairs'. Levels of autonomy differ between programmes but even independent producers are subject to hierarchical pressures. As one commented:

> Making a documentary is not a democratic process. Even if you're an independent [producer] the money is put up by someone and at the end of the day they have the final decision. They are usually the broadcaster and I think you should never forget that.

These 'final' decisions can focus upon perceived audience needs, and producers may face pressures over content, title or even the accompanying press release. One producer who made a factual film about a psychiatric institution outlines her negative experience of organisational hierarchy:

> I think that hierarchically there are pressures to do with content. I did make one documentary where someone very senior said 'It's not shocking enough. It's just not shocking enough'. And it was at a viewing and they felt I hadn't made, to put it crudely, as much as I could have done of the material, so against my will it was made more shocking and one of the senior bosses said 'Look, the switchboard should be jammed after this programme, it should be absolutely jammed' and I found that very difficult. He wasn't necessarily being negative. He might have been saying, 'We want outrage because this is an outrageous situation and this is why we made the documentary' but on the other hand I felt the absolute pressure to make it more shocking was questionable.

Decisions around the title of a programme are crucial because a 'sexy' title can attract previewers, who in turn attract audiences. The same producer was pressured 'from above' to retitle two documentaries on mental illness simply to increase the audience 'hype':

> That seems of significance because the broadcasters want a title that will catch the eye of newspaper journalists and previewers. So I have had two experiences where I didn't agree at all [with the titles] and I had tried very hard to make these documentaries low key because the material was so awful and people's stories were so tragic but on the other hand I know that calling it by a hyped-up title does increase the hype, you probably get more previews.

The well-received comedy drama *Takin' Over the Asylum* was also retitled in accordance with anticipated viewer reaction. Audience research found that potential viewers preferred *Takin' Over the Asylum* to the original title *Making Waves*. The programme, however, failed to attract large audiences. The decision to alter the title was not made by the writer but between the producer and controller for BBC2. As the producer explains here, he believes it was the subject rather than the title which was responsible for low viewing figures:

The real problem for me was that such a wonderful show was watched by such a small proportion of the television viewing audience [and] I'll take full responsibility for [changing the title] because I was the producer and certainly when we researched the different titles the one that we ended up with was the one which got the most positive response from the likely television viewing audience. I think there was what would appear to be at first sight a difficult subject matter and a real problem of convincing a large audience that they should conquer it.

The content of press releases to accompany future programmes is also designed to attract previewers and audiences. One documentary producer had written her own press release, which she described as 'a bit boring but accurate'. However, the press department of the broadcasting institution re-wrote the press release to increase public attention. The producer concluded by saying: 'whether in the end more people watched the programme or not I don't know but the pressure to get ratings, to get people to watch these documentaries, is very definitely there'.

The clear need for gripping visuals is a constant concern for producers and can lead to tension with medical staff. Producers, under constant pressure to find 'televisual' moments, can have their efforts blocked by medical professionals who may veto access to distressed patients. There appears to be two inherent problems. First, the medical profession lacks respect for the media profession and second, medical staff simply do not understand 'the nature of television'. One producer clashed with medical staff over the filming of scenes which were considered to be particularly intrusive to patient's privacy. In this producer's view, the medical profession fail to comprehend the medium of television and the needs of audiences. As she concluded:

You are making television and you're making something which has to attract people to watch it otherwise you've failed in everything you have tried to do and it's the nature of the beast. It has to hold people. It has to be something you switch on and you become absorbed in and the only way to do that is to use particular techniques, you have cliff-hangers.

The need for dramatic visual moments not only affects the ways in which people with mental health problems are represented when they are ill, but also crucially how they are represented when they are well.

Portraying mental health

This issue is of key concern to campaigning groups. One of their main complaints is that often well-intentioned portrayals of people in mental distress can fall into the 'cup of tea' syndrome. Portraying someone making a cup of tea thus symbolises normality. The criticism is that this image hardly serves to change the impression of service users as helpless victims. The makers of television, with their dependency on dramatic visual moments, will happily feature people in crisis but when these people recover from their illness, production teams struggle to make 'good television' out of normality. One producer explained that unless you are making a 'training piece for television' it is exceptionally difficult to represent mental health visually:

> For us it was much more interesting when someone had a crisis because it was much better television than the fifth or sixth therapy session where they are talking to their worker, you know it just doesn't make television and the being ill process is kind of interesting for nearly all the time that someone's ill. When they start to get better it's only interesting in bits [...] you don't want to film it all and it was very difficult because a lot of people thought that we lost interest in them when we had to start tailing off the filming.

This comes perilously close to voyeurism in relation to the mentally ill. It also raises important ethical questions about the effect of featuring people in a way which makes them feel that TV was interested in them only when they were behaving 'oddly'. Being 'well' does not apparently command the same attention:

> Being well is dead boring because mostly people are much more interesting when they're ill. They just are. We tried to find seminal events but largely we would end up with them in their homes or them in the park. It's a real problem actually. There's no way we're ever going to be able to show people well because it's not good television. I mean it's good training but it's not telly and often it is a limitation that television is a medium that we most frequently use to allow people to meet people who are mentally ill because television is a very specific medium. We don't have a mass medium which doesn't depend on being involving, like having a story or some kind of structure.

In the end, budgetary constraints may also be a key factor here. There clearly are very many positive and dynamic images of mental health which could be featured rather than simply 'walking around a park'. Organisations such as the Scottish Association for Mental Health run training programmes in areas such as new technology and computing skills, where people can very obviously be seen to be regaining control over their own lives. Other organisations of users of services have been formed specifically to challenge 'passive' and victim-focused images of mental illness.

Taking words out of people's mouths

Producers themselves may be personally committed to presenting more positive or sympathetic images of mental ill health but organisational pressures can overrule this concern. For example, one producer believed very strongly that patients should speak for themselves, to balance the negative visual content of her film series. Pressure 'from above' dictated that the patients' stories were given by 'voice-over'. This producer pointed out that it is only fairly recently that it has been viewed as 'politically correct' for the medium of television to give a voice to disempowered individuals and acknowledges the 'survivor/victim' dilemma as highly problematic:

It is a massive problem in this area. For example, when I was making one of these films, visually some of the people looked absolutely terrible as if they had been absolutely wiped out by their experience of incarceration. Now, I knew that they hadn't been wiped out by it and I would have preferred to have given them more time to speak in their words but then I was put under pressure to put their stories in the commentary and I felt that would give the impression that these people couldn't speak for themselves.

There are clear factors which influence decision-making over how interviewees' stories are presented in the documentary format. Most simply, it is far quicker to paraphrase someone else's story which can be made to 'fit' with the overall programme agenda: 'you can make them say more or less exactly what you want them to say'. Another significant concern is that the story should be made easily comprehensible for audiences. As a producer described:

I was told more than once either that the person speaking wasn't making sense or that the audience wouldn't be able to understand – if this was the case of course you could deal with it in subtitles – this allows the person to speak for themselves but it still takes more time than a voice-over written by someone else.

This particular producer overcame such problems by using a combination of methods. Her films did use voice-over to paraphrase the person's story but intercut this with footage of individuals telling their own stories.

Production values play a key role in decision-making here. For example, by using voice-over the film avoids being labelled as 'worthy' or being perceived as 'access TV', where the production does not have complete editorial control. The 'house style' of both the production company making the series and the broadcast channel will also dictate the extent to which people speak for themselves. Thus perceptions of how the audience 'wants its information' and 'what it is capable of grasping' are used to justify the paraphrasing of personal speech. An added concern is that for the production company, the use of commentary facilitates a constant 'authority' voice for viewers. As this producer explains further: 'The more voice-over you have in proportion to the interviewees, the easier it is to transmit your own authority, easier too to remind the audience "we did this", "revealed that", put your own stamp on the film.'

Problems about access and representation in media are not confined to the field of mental health but extend to other disempowered or minority groups. However, if public perceptions of people who have experienced mental distress are to change positively, it seems crucial that these individuals are allowed the space and time to speak for themselves.

Media impact on users of services

The very presence of a television production crew in a psychiatric institution can influence the behaviour of patients. The producers we interviewed were highly aware of this impact, particularly with respect to some people who were severely disturbed. One producer recalled her experience of filming four days each week within a hospital:

> We were doing things that fed into their illness. Like one chap had paranoid delusions and he completely felt that the hospital was out to get him and he was frightened to death and he thought he had hired this film crew to record every instance in order to keep the hospital on their toes. In some cases there were people who thought there were cameras in every room. There was one chap who thought that cameras were following him and the doctor said 'But they are!'.

Often a producer is faced with a conflict between contributing to someone's distress and making a film which has maximum visual impact. Decision-making here rests entirely upon the personal integrity of the producer. One producer explains why the very subject of mental illness may present a dilemma for 'media people' in particular:

> It's really hard for people who [work in] media and what you're looking for is the intensity and drama because that's what makes good television, so it's incredibly hard not to get seduced by that initially and I actually think its far too easy to wind someone up, someone who has delusions or psychosis and you're creating something in their head, and of course for you it's great telly and there were a couple of occasions where I think we came too close to that.

Again economic restraints play a major role in such decisions. One producer outlined how the production budget determines your flexibility over such issues. A producer is unlikely to have the 'luxury' of losing valuable footage given that the majority of documentary films on mental illness must be completed within two or three weeks. As she says: 'If I had been making that film over a limited period of time I would have had to carry on [with the interview] or at least I would have felt I had to carry on because you can't waste filming days. They are far too expensive.' On some occasions this producer did allow film to be transmitted which included someone who was obviously reacting to the cameras. The decision was taken to screen such scenes to illustrate the effect of the filming process on individuals:

> One thing I don't really think we disinterred was the effect we were having on them [the patients] and occasionally it comes through where in one scene one of the women is having a very manic high and you know it is just for the cameras but that was the sort of thing we wanted to keep in to say there is a level of this going on.

Factors which condition more positive portrayals

There are, however, spaces where more positive or 'realistic' representations of mental illness can occur. It is important to examine the values which underpin these portrayals. In our analysis of media output (see Chapter 4) we found that the BBC hospital drama series *Casualty* produced sympathetic items on mental illness. To understand this it is crucial to examine the way in which *Casualty* storylines are 'worked through' from ideas stage to final draft.

Casualty places high value on background research. This is not simply in terms of reading newspaper cuttings or medical journals but also includes practical experience where writers visit hospital departments to observe patients and discuss cases with medical staff. A script-editor for the programme explains this prioritising of personal research:

> What is absolutely fundamental is that the writer really researches the story. At the end of the day *Casualty* is a research drama. It has to have that credibility about it. We would always encourage new writers to go to a casualty department anywhere in the country.

Casualty writers are not only encouraged to find their own contacts in the medical or social services profession but are also supported by regular medical advisers on the programme. An experienced female writer describes her first experience of becoming involved: 'I got my first commission [for *Casualty*] and then went off and researched it in my local hospitals, Guys, Greenwich, I just spent a night and observed, watched cases, talked to the nurses.' The programme also paid a consultancy fee to allow her to discuss a future abortion storyline with a gynaecologist.

At an organisational level *Casualty* has regular medical advisers to the production team. Thus from the earliest stage a storyline will be checked for inaccuracies. As a script-editor outlines here, the script is from initial conception liable to be scrapped if it is factually inaccurate:

> We have three medical advisers so they are on hand and obviously at the [initial] stage it is very important that the medical advisers give the stories the thumbs up ... often we would have cases where a medical adviser would say 'this would never happen' so obviously we chuck the story out. Every single stage goes to a medical adviser for checks on dialogue ... once we've had all the medical notes back and the producer's notes and the script-editor's notes we then have a meeting with the writer and they go away and rewrite again. ... Even when a script has been finalised there are usually changes. A doctor might say, 'Well actually he wouldn't say or do that'.

An additional factor which may influence the factual quality of scripts on other programmes is the relative pressure of 'deadlines'. A *Casualty* writer saw this as a crucial factor which is often overlooked. She believes that the pressure of deadlines is less immediate for *Casualty* writers, which can again have an impact on the accuracy of portrayals:

> The beauty of *Casualty* is the amount of freedom you have, which you have on *The Bill* also but they're putting out so much more that they have to be tighter with it and [on *Casualty*] there's quite a lot more time so you are able to rush around and find out about your subject much more.

Personal experience/advice from mental health organisations

Another programme which provides a useful example of more positive media portrayals is the BBC comedy drama *Takin' Over the Asylum*. Again, it is possible to identify factors which clearly contributed to this.

More balanced images of mental illness do not simply arise from the input of the medical profession. Personal experience of mental distress or advice from campaigning groups can also result in more accurate or balanced media portrayals. *Takin' Over the Asylum* was a fairly radical approach to the portrayal of mental illness. In our audience groups it was praised by mental health service users for depicting psychiatric patients as articulate and humorous. The programme had a deliberate agenda to challenge public misconceptions of the subject. The writer herself had direct experience of mental distress and was acutely aware of the problems in this field. She also took special advice from campaigning groups on mental health. As the producer of the programme (now BBC Head of Drama Series) recalls:

> Although that area is regularly visited in television drama, that particular approach is not and the sheer involvement of [the writer] is very unusual. [The writer] worked closely with mental health organisations, especially SAMH (Scottish Association for Mental Health) and that was an important thing.

Another factor which cannot be overestimated is support for a writer from within the broadcasting hierarchy. The programme's producer supported the writer's aim to challenge existing perceptions of mental illness. As he outlines here:

> I think the serial did an extraordinary amount for people who watched it in changing perceptions ... there are very few things that got the same reaction from people [with mental health problems] and who derived a complicated comfort from the programme. Donna [Franceschild] had such a strong line to the mental health organisations that I for myself trusted what she was doing. She was committed to them in a basic way.

The commitment of those involved in the production and the support from within the broadcast hierarchy combined to ensure that the programme succeeded in challenging negative attitudes to psychiatric patients. This support may be rare but it does exist. An independent producer who has for many years been concerned with changing the media image of mental illness sees hierarchical support as of fundamental importance. With her two most recent films she was given this support. This meant that in terms of content she had relative autonomy to present the kind of 'low key' image that she wanted and was not 'under any pressure at all to dramatise or up the hype in terms of the material'. As she explains further:

> I think there are interested people in the hierarchy in television who think that to have been institutionalised for 60 years is a quiet and terrible drama in its own right and to have a woman sit in front of a camera is as dramatic as anything you can cobble together.

Conclusion

In this chapter I have identified a series of factors which may influence how mental health is represented in 'non-news' television programming. The aim is not to provide 'excuses' for media personnel but rather to illustrate that the production process is a complex one. Production workers operate in an intense environment where organisational and economic pressures are constant. In this climate, underlying assumptions about audience needs can subordinate other concerns and result in distorted and misleading images. Writers and producers are not, however, autonomous and overall responsibility rests with those further up the broadcast hierarchy. Support from within this hierarchy can ensure that more challenging portrayals of mental health are produced. Equally, as has been illustrated, organisational power structures can override the personal commitment of writers and producers to this area.

In the current climate of increasing competition between channels some producers who took part in the study did voice fears that perceptions of audience needs will play a greater role in the decision-making process. As television becomes further consumer-orientated, the types of subject matter and, more crucially, the ways in which this material is framed, could become even more tightly managed. If campaigning groups are to expand the limited range of images which currently exist then it is crucial that they understand the nature of media production. Strategies for intervention will be more succesful if they take account of the underlying media values which condition representations in this area. Groups can challenge these stigmatising images by adopting proactive measures. By such groups advising on or taking part in television programming dominant myths and stereotypes about mental illness can be challenged. However, if public misconceptions of mental health are to be truly changed, service users must also gain access to making their own representations. In the words of one documentary maker who has campaigned for more positive images of mental health: 'Television can make the visible invisible.' Those who have experienced mental distress are likely to remain 'invisible' unless they become active participants in the production process and use the medium of television to create images of themselves.

CHAPTER 3

A sense of perspective: the media and the Boyd Inquiry

David Crepaz-Keay

Context

'The Confidential Inquiry into Homicides and Suicides by Mentally Ill People' was set up in 1991 following a small number of high profile cases in which people who had been diagnosed mentally ill had killed themselves or others. The inquiry was directed by Dr William Boyd, Consultant Psychiatrist and a former Vice-Chairman of the Mental Welfare Commission for Scotland, and was chaired by Professor Andrew Sims, the then President of the Royal College of Psychiatrists. This coincided with the high profile of the policy of shifting mental health services from institutions to community-based resources. This policy of shifting services was by no means new, nor had it been particularly swift (at the time the inquiry was set up, two-thirds of money spent on mental health services was spent on in-patient care), but the publication of the Department of Health's *Caring for People* (1989) and the introduction of the care programme approach meant that the policy of community care was under close scrutiny. In August 1994, the Inquiry published its preliminary report (Confidential Inquiry 1994). This chapter examines the media coverage which this report received.

The report

The cases the inquiry team looked at were homicides committed in England and Wales by people who had been in contact with specialist psychiatric services in the 12 months prior to the death. The number of cases fitting this remit during the three years 1991–1993 that the inquiry covered was 34. The committee found no other homicides by such people during those three years. It is not impossible that there were other homicides by people in touch with psychiatric services, but the figure of 34 (or just less than one a month, on average) is the best figure available. During the same period, about 2,000 homicides (or about 55 each month) occurred in England and Wales. The homicides committed by people recently in contact with psychiatric services, therefore, represent only a tiny proportion of those committed in any given year. Nor should it be assumed that these homicides were a result of any mental illness.

The inquiry team then tried to examine each of the 34 cases in detail. For a variety of reasons, from legal to organisational, it was not possible to follow up each case. The detail of the report was, therefore, based on an in-depth study of 22 cases, the equivalent of two years worth of data.

The media expressed fears of 'schizophrenics' (the images were often of Black schizophrenics) being let out of hospital, defaulting on their medication, and killing strangers. The report showed a different picture. Only about a third of those killing had a diagnosis of schizophrenia, about a quarter had a diagnosis of manic depression, and the vast majority were Caucasian.

As is true of homicides in general, the victims of people who had used psychiatric services tended to be known to them. Fewer than one in 10 of the incidents involved the killing of a stranger. If there was a striking feature of the report, it was that over a quarter of the incidents were mothers killing their young children.

The report showed that less than half of the people who committed the homicides had been discharged from hospital in the year prior to the offence. It told us that more than three-quarters of those killing were receiving the level of supervision that their professionals thought appropriate. Indeed a significant number, almost a quarter, had been seen in the 24 hours leading to the incident. And though the report mentioned that some people had defaulted on recommended treatment, the figures showed that only a few of those who killed had failed to take prescribed medication. It seems ironic, in the light of the press coverage, that three-quarters of those who killed had complied with prescribed medication. When *A Preliminary Report on Homicide* was published, it provided additional evidence for a well-informed discussion on continuing the move from institution to community that could move beyond the 'psycho-killer' coverage that had dogged 'community care' up to that point. Unfortunately, the coverage that accompanied the report did nothing to allay public concern.

The headlines

The media greeted the report as follows: '33 patients freed to kill' (*Daily Express*, 17 August, p. 1); '"Care in the community" mental patients kill 34 people in 18 months' (*The Times*, 17 August, p. 5); 'One murder a fortnight by mentally ill' (*Daily Telegraph*, 17 August, p. 1); 'Insane killers' (*Evening Standard*, 17 August, p. 9) 'Scandal of loonies freed to kill' (*Daily Star*, 18 August, p. 8); 'Sick and dangerous' (*Daily Mail* , 18 August, p. 8); 'Free to kill' (*The Sun* , 18 August, p. 6).

The headlines, and the more than two hundred column inches of reporting devoted to the report offer an excellent study in the way the British media treats mental health. This analysis will look in some detail at the content of *A Preliminary Report on Homicide*, and how it was reported in the newspapers of the 17th and 18th of August 1994 and on the television news broadcast throughout the 17th August.

Factual inaccuracies

The most glaring problem with the press coverage in most papers was a simple one of numerical inaccuracy which led to nearly all newspapers doubling the frequency of homicides. Some of this was undoubtedly made worse by the ambiguity of the press release from the Department of Health. This gave the impression that the 34 homicides occurred during the 18 month lifespan of the inquiry's work on the preliminary report. This offers little excuse, however, particularly for the *Evening Standard* of 17 August and all reports of 18 August as the Health Minister, John Bowis, had made the frequency clear on numerous broadcast interviews.

The *Daily Telegraph*'s (17 August) front page headline 'One murder a fortnight by mentally ill', sub headed 'Call for compulsory medication after 34 killings in 18 months' was the most prominent example of this. The report beneath the headline repeats the error twice. The *Times*'s '"Care in the community" mental patients kill 34 in 18 months' also repeats the error in the text. The *Daily Express*'s front page headline '33 patients freed to kill' is followed by 'The toll in 18 months ...'. The 34 deaths in 18 months error is repeated in reports from the *Evening Standard* (pp. 6 and 9), and the following day by the *Guardian* (p. 4), the *Daily Star* (p. 8), and *The Sun* (pp. 2 and 6) '... at the horrifying rate of one a fortnight', while the *Morning Star* (p. 3) produced an otherwise unreported figure of 22 killings in 18 months.

The Times repeated its error of the day before on a page 2 article on the 18th. But the *Daily Telegraph* topped its four quotes of the wrong figure on the 17th by using its own 'one murder a fortnight' headline in the masthead for a full-page article by Majorie Wallace, introduced with the predictably inaccurate, 'In 18 months, 34 people have been murdered by the mentally ill. The figures show that care in the community is a sham'. The article then repeats the error once more.

It is worth mentioning that of the newspapers covering the report, only the *Daily Mail* and the *Independent* were accurate in their reporting of the incidence of homicides. Both carried extensive coverage, but neither felt the need to double the data. BBC and ITN did not emerge with much greater credit for accuracy. ITN's 12.30 p.m. lunch-time bulletin opened their item on the report with the figure of 34 in 18 months. This was later corrected by the Minister for Health, John Bowis. The BBC's *One O'Clock News* also headlined with 34 in 18 months, which was also corrected by John Bowis in interview. The BBC then managed to revert to the 34 in 18 months figure for their closing headlines! By teatime, ITN had the correct figure for their introduction to the story. By the end of the 5.40 bulletin, however, the closing headlines gave us one killing a fortnight.

Medication

In the analysis of the 22 cases that could be examined in depth, questions were asked about compliance with medication and treatment. In psychiatry, treatment could mean anything from electro-convulsive therapy (ECT) to attending a drop-in centre. The inquiry found that of the 22, five were not taking prescribed medication and one had failed to attend for a regular injection of medication. In addition to the six out of 22 who had refused medication, two had failed to keep outpatient appointments, one had refused inpatient care, three had refused to consider outpatient supervision, and one had denied her community psychiatric nurse access to her home. Compliance with medication was therefore an issue in six cases (27 per cent) and other treatments in a further seven (32 per cent). Though this amounts to 13 (59 per cent) in total, there is an important distinction between drugs and other medical treatments when calls are made for compulsory medication. The drugs prescribed by psychiatrists can be damaging and there are many good reasons why people choose not to take it. This has little to do with the level of support people need in the community, and it is the support that is likely to reduce the risk of violent incidents.

The *Daily Express* front page piece (17 August) stated 'Most violence happened because the attackers failed to take their medication'; the *Daily Telegraph* (18th, p. 4) stated 'more than half the mentally ill patients who committed murder in the past 18 months did so after failing to take their prescribed medication'. The *Guardian's* comment (18th, p. 21) was 'The one common theme in the cases under review was failure on the part of those who killed to keep appointments or to take the drugs prescribed for them' (common in that 13 didn't and 9 did). *The Times* (17th, p. 5) agreed, 'All of them had failed to take medication or had missed medical appointments before they killed.'

The *Daily Mail* (17th, p. 11) said that 'more than half had been refusing medical treatment after leaving hospital'. Medical treatment, rather than just treatment, seems to imply medication, particularly when read with their comment entitled 'Sick and dangerous' (18th, p. 8): 'If they neglect to take proper medication, mentally sick people released into the community can be a danger to others.' Few could match, however, 'The Sun Says' (18th, p. 6) under the title 'Free to kill': 'They go berserk because they don't take essential medication ...'.

The BBC News coverage was similarly loose with its headlines. In the *One O'Clock News*, the BBC opened the item with '[the report] established in over half the cases examined in detail, patients had failed to take their prescribed medication'. The BBC report underlined this error by looking at the case of Andrew Robinson, a person diagnosed as having schizophrenia, who killed an occupational therapist, Georgina

Robinson (no relation). The BBC mysteriously failed to mention that Andrew Robinson was receiving depot (i.e. injected) medication for at least three months prior to the homicide, so his compliance with medication cannot have been in doubt. By the *Nine O'Clock News*, this had moderated to 'The report found that *many* had failed to take prescribed medication.' Whether six amounts to many is, however, still questionable.

The net

One of the most commonly uttered phrases by the Secretary of State for Health at the time, Virginia Bottomley, referred to people 'falling through the net of care'. The idea of *the net of care* was originally in the context of a safety net, and though this is clearly so in the *Morning Star*'s piece 'Complacency at killings condemned' (18 August, p. 3) which describes 'patients who had slipped through the care in the community safety net ...', The *Daily Mail*'s interpretation was somewhat different. With its sub-heading 'Ex-patients escape the care "net"' (17th, p. 11), the *net* is clearly one that is designed for trapping rather than supporting. Following this theme, the call was for stronger supervision. This ranged from the *Guardian*'s '13 [murders] might have been avoided had the patients been kept under closer medical supervision' (18th, p. 21 Comment), to the *Daily Telegraph*'s call for 'compulsory medication of patients who do not take their prescribed medication, and their enforced return to hospital' (18th, p. 17). But what does the report actually say about the level of supervision received?

Two of the 22 people who committed the homicides (9 per cent) were being seen daily, six (27 per cent) weekly and another two (9 per cent) monthly. More interestingly, five people (22 per cent) had been seen in the 24 hours prior to the killing, another six (27 per cent) were seen during the previous month, and six (27 per cent) more were having 'continuing regular contact based on their perceived needs'. So half the people who killed had been seen in the month prior to the event, and fewer than one in four were being seen less frequently than the professionals must have judged was necessary.

When asked explicitly about the value of compulsory supervision under mental health legislation the professionals involved in the cases indicated; that even in retrospect, 'the possibility had only been considered of possible relevance in two cases'. The evidence of the Boyd inquiry simply does not support the popular media view of a large number of mentally ill people being 'freed' to kill.

Freed to kill

The idea of 'escaping' forms the basis of the overriding impression, given by the way the report was portrayed, that the policy of community care is one of taking a homogenous group of people who are danger-ously mentally ill and securely locked in psychiatric hospitals, and simply placing them in the community at large, where they could kill innocent people at will. The reality of community care is somewhat different, of course.

The headlines promoting this impression fall into two categories. The first is typified by *The Times*'s '"Care in the community" mental patients kill 34 in 18 months', and the *Guardian*'s 'Death and care in the com-munity', reinforcing the impression that there is a strong causal link between the homicides and the policy.

The second, and far more common and worrying type of 'escaping' headline is the 'freed to kill' variety. It is typified by the *Daily Express*'s '33 Patients freed to kill' (17 August, front page), and echoed by the *Evening Standard*'s 'Row grows over freedom for danger patients' (17th, p. 6), *The Sun*'s 'Mum's fury over freed killers' (18th, p. 2) and 'Free to kill' (p. 6), and the *Daily Star*'s 'Scandal of loonies freed to kill' (18th, p. 8).

This impression can be compared with what the report reveals about the people committing murder. The idea of psychiatric hospi-tals decanting populations of lunatics into the community at large, and these people going out and killing is unsupported. Nothing in the report suggests that these people should (or would, prior to 'com-munity care') have been kept in hospital for life. Of the 22 cases explored, one person was an inpatient at the time of the homicide, reinforcing the fact that hospitalisation is not a guarantee of safety. Two people had been discharged from specialist care altogether within the year, it seems unlikely that they would have been kept in hospital if professionals believed that they needed no psychiatric care at all. Six of the people had a diagnosis of manic depression. Again, the likelihood of people with this diagnosis being kept in hospital for life is remote.

The area of the report that tells us most about the 'freed to kill' myth is that which explores the psychiatric care people were receiving in the 'episode of illness', that is to say what was the nature of their most recent contact with psychiatric services.

The first aspect of care worth looking at is use of detention under the 1983 Mental Health Act. This gives a good indication of what level of security and compulsion professionals deemed appropriate for the people in question, and hence insight into the perceived risk of any degree of independence for these individuals. In only three of the 22 cases studied (14 per cent), were people thus detained. A further seven (32 per cent) had spent some time during their most recent contact as a patient in hospital. So 12 people (55 per cent) had not even been a patient in hospital at all in the 12 months prior to the homicide. This is hardly, therefore, a predominantly hospital-based population moving (or being released/freed) into the broader community to commit murder.

It is important to add to this that one cannot blame the closing of hos-pitals for the fact that these people were not admitted. Despite direct questioning in relation to availability of in-patient facilities, professionals made no complaints that admission had been prevented by bed shortages. This is an important fact to remember, particularly when considering the media's proposed solutions to their perceived problem of the psycho-killer on the loose.

What should be done?

There is no shortage of advice to help deal with the problem, even if the incorrect way in which it is understood has been created by the media itself.

While some call for compulsory medication (though only about a quarter of those studied in detail had been found to be refusing what was prescribed), the most frequent call was for people to be kept in hospital.

The Sun, the *Daily Star*, *Today*, the *Daily Mail*, the *Daily Express*, the *Independent* and the *Daily Telegraph* all had articles calling for more and/ or longer hospitalisation despite the fact that fewer than half of those who killed had actually been in hospital in the year prior to the act.

Conclusions

No one would deny that the homicides by people who had used psychiatric services were tragic for all involved, nor should anyone suggest that reasonable steps ought not to be taken to avoid the avoidable. For example, there is a clear need for distressed people and their families to be taken seriously when they seek help and for that help to be more readily available in the community. But infrequent and isolated events should not be used by all sections of the media to damn an entire group of people. The deaths were in fact a very small proportion of homicides as a whole, and those who killed were a tiny proportion of those who are mentally distressed. The deaths could not be attributed to a policy of 'releasing' into the community large numbers of 'dangerous' people who refused to take their medication and killed at random.

When the media were presented with simple reliable information to criticise such stereotypes it was often either ignored or inaccurately reported. This is not just the irresponsibility for which the tabloid newspapers are justly famous. It is an irresponsibility that was repeated in almost every quality paper, and on both BBC and independent television; it is one that leaves the vast majority of the public in ignorance, and those of us with a psychiatric diagnosis under a cloud of suspicion.

It is more important than ever that people are allowed to become part of the community. It is also vitally important that mental health professionals engage, and gain the trust of, people who need services. For these things to happen, people need to be well informed. This report offered an unprecedented opportunity for the false perceptions of a necessary link between a diagnosis of mental illness and violence to be dashed and to criticise some of the most popular myths about the community care programme. The newspapers and television news blew that chance, and ignored the truth, for the sake of a story.

CHAPTER 4

Media content

Greg Philo, Greg McLaughlin and Lesley Henderson

This chapter is based on the content analysis of media coverage of mental illness, focusing on news reports, fictional television, popular magazines and children's literature.

The sample comprised a range of national and local media output for the month of April 1993 and includes both factual and fictional representations. Factual formats in the press include news items, comment and analysis. For television we analysed news and relevant current affairs programmes. In magazines, we examined feature items, medical columns and problem pages. Fictional formats on television included soap operas, single dramas and films. In the press and magazines, they included short stories and comic strips. The specific content of the sample was as follows.

For television, we recorded the main evening news bulletins on BBC (*Nine O'Clock News*) and ITN (*The News at Ten*), as well as the children's programme *Newsround* (BBC). We also included the local TV news magazines on BBC Scotland (*Reporting Scotland*) and on Scottish Television (*Scotland Today*). Current affairs and documentary programmes were recorded whenever appropriate.

For children's programmes we included the Saturday morning magazine, *Going Live!* (BBC) and *What's Up Doc?* (ITV), for their cartoons, feature items and live entertainment spots. Our sample of fictional television included soap operas such as *Coronation Street*, *Brookside*, *EastEnders*, *Neighbours*, *Home And Away* and Scottish Television's *Take the High Road*. We recorded three medical drama series – *Casualty*, *Medics* and *Children's Ward* – as well as relevant single dramas and films.

For the press sample we focused on the tabloids, since they are a potential source of common-sense understandings and popular myths about social issues and have a very large audience. We included *The Sun, Daily Mirror, Daily Star, Daily Sport, Daily Record, Evening Times* (Glasgow), *Evening News* (Edinburgh), and the Scottish quality papers, the *Herald* and the *Scotsman*. The Sunday press sample included *News of the World*, the *People, Sunday Sport, Sunday Mail*, the *Sunday Post, Scottish*

Sunday Express, and *Scotland on Sunday.* The magazines in our sample were *Fastforward, Smash Hits, Big, Mizz, Take a Break, Bella, Best, Cosmopolitan, Woman, Woman's Own* and the two men's style magazines, *Arena* and *GQ.* Our sample also took in the children's comics *M & J, Jackie,* and the Sega computer games magazine, *Sega Power.*

We recorded/stored and analysed all of these for April 1993 and our quantitative assessments of different elements of their content are based on this month. But in some cases we extended our analysis beyond this period. In the case of soap operas, some storylines ran before and after the period and it was necessary to record extra programmes in order to analyse key themes as they developed. There was a second major reason to go outside the April period. Our audience groups were obviously not bound by it in terms of their own memories, so we needed to follow up references which they made to television programmes, films and news stories from outside the period.

Methodology

The purpose of this content analysis is to show the dominant messages which are being given about mental illness across a variety of media. In the texts which we analysed there was a very extensive use of words that related to mental illness. There was also a very wide range of stories in both fictional and non-fictional sources featuring people who are reported or shown as being 'mentally ill' (we include a lexicon of the terms used in Appendix 1). The usage varied from clinical/technical terms such as 'psychosis' and 'dementia', through to the popular language of the tabloid press such as 'deranged', 'pychopathic' and 'maniac'. An important point to note is the sheer penetration of such terms into everyday language. They are also used in descriptions which have nothing to do with mental illness, where the intention is simply to be negative or derogatory, as in 'the loony left' or 'motorway madness'. In this news feature from the *Guardian* (1 April 1993), a town is described using familiar (and incorrect) assumptions about schizophrenia to highlight the 'dividing' effect of a road: 'You don't even have to travel to the schizophrenic sprawl bisected by the North Circular Road – the concrete forest of Harlesden to the south and stippled semis of affluent Wembley to the north.'

There are also many references to being 'mad' or 'crazy' to describe eccentric behaviour. These are most prominent in material for young people. The intended sense is of being exciting or 'rule breaking'. For example, the *Daily Mirror* (4 May 1993) used this headline to increase the appeal of its exam revision guide: 'Good luck you bonkers loonies, and DON'T PANIC!' This is a further example of language which is obviously not intended to imply mental illness as such. The techniques of content analysis used here are designed to identify the heaviest carriers of meaning in both fictional and non-fictional texts. We show, for example, the range of themes that are present in news stories or soap operas and highlight the crucial pieces of language and visual images which are likely to have the most impact on audiences. Our earlier research has suggested that such language and imagery can have a crucial influence in forming ways of understanding and the development of social attitudes.

There are three dimensions to this part of our content analysis. First, the identification of explanatory or interpretative themes; second, the examination of the manner in which each theme is developed in a specific context; third, the assessment of the frequency with which different themes appear.

In the case of news stories we looked at the use of headlines and different types of news language, at how central characters in stories were labelled as 'mentally ill' and the types of actions with which they were associated. In the fictional material we looked at key story lines relating to mental illness and at the structure of plots and dramatic action. We show the manner in which these can promote attitudes and affective reactions among the audience towards the central characters of the drama. The structure of the plot and the relations between the characters in most soap operas establish very quickly who are to be seen as 'villains' to be reviled and who are meant to elicit our sympathy. In Chapter 5 of this volume we will show how successful such programmes actually are in producing intense reactions from their audience.

Discussion of results

In the first phase of the content analysis we grouped references to mental illness into the major categories. These are (1) 'comic' images; (2) violence/harm to others; (3) violence to self; (4) prescriptions for treatment/advice/recovery; (5) criticisms of accepted definitions of mental illness.

The bar charts in Figures 4.1a, 4.1b and 4.1c illustrate the number of news stories/ fictional portrayals and other items in each of the categories. It can be seen that there are many more items which relate violence to the mentally ill than those which present a more positive image. Such a count actually overestimates the impact of positive presentations since these are very largely composed of letters to problem pages and advice columns. By contrast the negative images are more likely to receive 'headline' treatment. Such issues can only be addressed by a more qualitative assessment of the content sample. We will go on to do this in relation to the five major categories.

Category 1: 'comic' images

These presentations can exploit any of a range of stereotypes about mentally ill people. For example, a political cartoon in *The Sun* (18

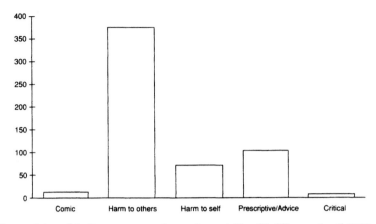

Figure 4.1a   Media representations of mental health/illness, April 1993.

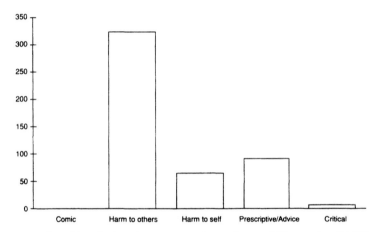

Figure 4.1b   Non-fictional representations of mental illness, April 1993.

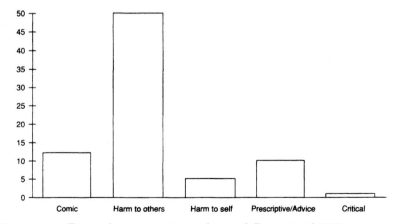

Figure 4.1c   Fictional representations of mental illness, April 1993.

March 1993), featured a psychiatric patient saying that Norman Lamont was doing a good job as the Conservative Chancellor. In the picture, a white-coated psychiatrist is commenting that the patient 'is our saddest case'. Around the group other patients are depicted dressed as Napoleon (see Appendix 2). Another image from the popular media is that of the mad scientist. For example, the ITV children's programme *What's Up Doc?* included one as its presenter, with dialogue such as: 'Everyone keeps picking on me just because I'm a psychopathic maniac devoted to unpleasant and useless research' (ITV, 9.30–11.30, 3 April 1993).

The Steve Wright Show (BBC Radio 1) has created a range of unusual characters for spoof interviews and commentaries. One is the 'paranoid man' who speaks in a strained voice and describes himself: 'I am not paranoid. It is they who spread rumours that I am using walkie talkies and infra-red beams' (15.00–15.45, 27 April 1993).

A more extended account of someone presented as mentally ill was given on Ruby Wax's show, *The Full Wax*. She introduced her show with these words:

> We have someone here with us tonight who recently joined the ranks of the chronically barking – the good news is that she has been rehabilitated via the miracle of 450 volts of electromagnetic currents zapping through your brain – this woman can now pick up BBC 2 simply by holding a fork.... I know you are going to be kind because if you are not she may pull a knife ... back from the abyss, Miss Joanna Lumley!

Joanna Lumley then appears, trembling and distressed, holding a place mat which she says she has made from her own hair and that 'this is a collage I made for Art Therapy and it is valium and some razor blades and I put on a bit of glitter because of the showbiz connection' (BBC1, 22.05, 22 April 1993). The finale of the show has Joanna Lumley dancing with men dressed in top hats and tails as they wrap her up in a straitjacket and carry her off out of the studio.

This show attracted some criticism after transmission. Anne Robinson on the BBC programme *Points of View* (BBC1, 20.50, 23 April 1993) commented on letters from people 'who felt mental illness was an inappropriate subject for a comedy show'. One of these stated that: 'For many thousands of people struggling to survive the pain of depression and anxiety the television allows them to keep in touch and relieve their loneliness.' The letter then refers to the show as a 'cheap jibe'. It is interesting that Ruby Wax is associated with alternative/progressive comedy (of the ilk of Jennifer Saunders/Rik Mayall etc.). It would be difficult to imagine anyone from this stable producing a parody of other stigmatised groups such as gays or Black people – for example, it would be *de rigeur* to avoid limp-wristed homosexual jokes. Yet it is 'acceptable' to parody the mentally ill, which indicates the importance of the campaigns to promote a more accurate portrayal of those who are mentally distressed and to raise the profile of their needs and rights.

Category 2: violence to others (factual representations)

This is a media world populated by 'psychopaths', 'maniacs' and 'frenzied knife men'. It has by far the largest number of items of all the categories. We found 323 news reports and other references which were presented as 'factual', and a further 50 from fictional sources. Such media images contrast sharply with the actualities of mental illness. Schizophrenia is typically associated with very confused thought processes and medical classifications do not even list violence as among its key symptoms. In reality only a small minority of people with serious mental illness are likely to be violent. The *Guardian* recently quoted a report from the National Schizophrenia Fellowship which showed that when violence did occur, it was very largely centred on family members:

> 75 per cent of all victims were closely related or in a close relationship with their attacker ... The mortal danger of these states [of mental illness] to outsiders does not appear to have been frequent. Only four cases on the NSF file indicate the killing of strangers. This is only a fraction of overall murder figures, and indeed a small proportion of the homicides in the 'Murder by Strangers' category. (*Guardian*, 10 April 1993)

But as we shall see, this is scarcely the picture which emerges from most of the popular media.

News and 'factual' references

We divided these into a series of sub-categories. The first was reports of attacks on strangers and the second assaults within families. The third dealt with harm to animals and the fourth sexual deviance/attacks. There was also at this time a wave of stories on the theme of 'psycho stalkers' who are obsessive fans or admirers. Finally the 'Waco siege' also occurred in the period of our sample. We have treated this as a separate category as it received a large amount of coverage with 157 items relating to it.

There were two other major stories which occurred just outside our sample but which we have given accounts of here. These are the 'Paris nursery school siege, 13–15 May, and the case of the nurse Beverley Allitt, convicted for murder on 17 May 1993.

Attacks on strangers
The story of a man attacking a woman and her daughter as they played bingo was widely reported by the press (5 April 1993) but with some qualitative differences. The headlines connote the extreme violence and horror of the incident:

KNIFEMAN HACKS GRAN TO DEATH AS SHE PLAYS BINGO

(Daily Star)

GRAN DIES IN BINGO HALL STAB TERROR – Knifeman runs amok
(Daily Sport)

MURDER AT BINGO – Women flee in terror as gran is hacked down
(The Sun)

BINGO HALL BLOODBATH   *(Daily Mirror)*

The circumstances of the attack were not made clear in reports and the police did not release the man's name to the press. However, *The Sun* and the *Daily Sport* both implied that the attacker may have been known to his victims. *The Sun* reported that the daughter had: 'recently moved in with [her mother] after [she] split with boyfriend Malcolm, 32. A 32 year-old man was being questioned last night'.

The attacker was described in these items as 'a knife maniac' and 'a madman' (*The Sun*), 'a crazed knife killer' and 'a maniac' (*Daily Star*). The *Daily Mirror* describes the man only as 'a knifeman' who 'launched a frenzied attack'. They also reported that the man laid down his weapon, walked 'drenched in blood' (the *Daily Sport*) to a nearby pub and calmly surrendered, saying 'The job's done'. *The Scotsman* reported the story in brief and without labelling. Its headline was simply:

MAN HELD AFTER DOUBLE STABBING

In a different story six days later, the *Sunday Sport* wrote of a 'psycho' woman in New Zealand who dressed up as a lollipop lady and beat pedestrians with her lollipop 'before running off, laughing hysterically':

PEDESTRIANS POLE-AXED BY CRAZED LOLLIPOP LADY
(Sunday Sport, 11 April 1993)

The newspaper described the woman as a 'potty pensioner' in her late sixties who had run her 'campaign of terror' for three weeks without being caught. It quotes the police saying they regarded the reports as a joke at first before realising 'she was very dangerous and had to be found'.

On 16 April a story appeared about a 'random attack' on a young boy. He claimed that a man poured petrol in his face and set fire to him. The *Daily Mirror* gave it front page prominence with large headlines and a photo of the victim taken before the attack:

SET ON FIRE BY A MANIAC – Hunt for fiend who tried to burn the face off Derek, 7

Four other newspapers also reported the story:

COPS HUNT MANIAC WHO TORCHED BOY, 7   *(Daily Record)*

EVIL 'DRUNK' SETS FIRE TO BOY'S FACE   *(The Sun)*

PARK LIGHTER FIEND IS HUNTED   *(Daily Star)*

MANIAC SETS LITTLE BOY'S FACE ON FIRE   *(Daily Sport)*

The young boy and his friend gave a detailed description of the man as having a scar on his face, a gold tooth, and smelling of drink (*Daily Mirror, Daily Record, Daily Sport*). The *Daily Mirror* and *Daily Record* quoted the police saying they were looking for 'a maniac ... some sort of lunatic who could do this'. However, an eyewitness later reported to the police that she saw the boys set fire to a can of petrol. The story had been made up to save them from getting into trouble. The *Daily Star* did not report this retraction. The *Daily Mirror* had featured it as a front page story, yet its retraction was printed as a short item on page 13.

This is an important story for our study since we used it later in our work with audience groups. As we shall see, the overall effect of the story was to perpetrate a completely false account.

On 19 April, the *Daily Sport* reported the murder of an old couple and their disabled son. They were beaten and stabbed to death in their home by young people, some 'as young as 14'. The headline was:

SICKO KIDS BLAMED FOR BLOODBATH THAT WIPED OUT FAMILY

A criminologist was reported to have 'built up a picture of the sick killers' minds' and told the paper that: 'The people who did this came to enjoy what they did towards the end.'

Violent attacks within families

Three newspapers reported the trial of a young woman who attempted to drown her baby daughter in the Thames (*Daily Star* 1 April 1993; the *Herald* and the *Scotsman* 2 April 1993). The *Daily Star* reported the penultimate day of the trial and clearly stated that she was mentally ill: 'Clarke, diagnosed a paranoid schizophrenic, admits tossing the baby from the bridge but denies attempted murder.' The woman was found 'not guilty by reason of insanity' and sent for treatment in mental hospital for an indeterminate period. The *Herald* and the *Scotsman* reported that the jury had been told there was no dispute about what the woman had done: 'What it had to decide was her state of mind at the time' (2 April 1993).

On 6 April, the *Daily Sport* reported how a mother attacked her two sons, stabbing and nearly killing one of them:

'WE LOVE YOU' STAB BOY TOLD HIS MUM – Fury sparked by Lego Brick

She was reported in court as having 'suffered from a manic depressive condition since she was 21'. The newspaper quoted the defence description of her attack as that of 'a deeply troubled mind at its lowest ebb'. Although put on probation for two years, she was ordered to 'get treatment for manic depressive psychosis'.

The *Daily Star* (28 April 1993) reported how a man in Germany killed his daughter and her partner after she refused to end the relationship. The headline was:

EVIL DAD KILLS DEFIANT DAUGHTER AND LOVER – He blasts them in busy street

The man was a Moslem from Jordan and objected to his daughter living with a non-Moslem from the West. The report did not describe him as mentally ill but cited an eyewitness: 'There was blood spattered everywhere – on shop-fronts and the pavement. This guy just flipped and turned into some kind of Rambo maniac.'

Attacks on animals
There were three reports on cruelty to animals. Two of these concerned specific attacks on horses:

MARE HURT BY SADIST   (The *People*, 11 April 1993)

AXE MANIAC IN ATTACK ON PET PONY   (*The Sun*, 14 April 1993)

Another reported an increase in Britain of cruelty to animals, with statistical details compiled by the RSPCA:

PET SADISTS HIT NEW LOW   (*Daily Sport*, 6 April 1993)

Sexual deviance/attacks
Some reports in the sample dealt with disturbed children. The *Daily Star* (16 April 1993) reported on a 'Sex pest aged six' who was expelled from his school for sexual harassment of pupils and teachers: 'School chiefs … have given the infant terror a special tutor who specialises in helping emotionally disturbed kids.'
On 20 April, four tabloids reported the conviction of a man who simulated sex on the street:

PERVERT HAD SEX WITH PAVEMENTS   (*Daily Record*)

JAIL FOR PAVEMENT PERVERT   (*Daily Mirror*)

FOOTPATH SEX KINK IS JAILED   (*Daily Sport*)

PAVEMENT PERVERT IS KERBED   (*The Sun*)

The man was imprisoned for 18 months on charges of 'outraging public decency'. The *Daily Record* quoted the judge who described him as 'a danger to the public [who] had a fetish he could not control'. All the reports mentioned that he had been ridiculed by other prisoners while on remand but only the *Daily Record* reported that he had tried to commit suicide as a result of this treatment. *The Sun's* version of the story was by the columnist Rikki Brown who used it as a vehicle for his 'humour':

At least he practised safe sex by wearing a traffic cone. His defence lawyer said [the man] had been nicknamed the Roadrumper by inmates in the remand centre. I'm not surprised. This is the man who gave the phrase, 'I'm just going up the road' a whole new meaning. I'm being tasteful here. I have no intention of doing the crack in the pavement joke or mentioning kerb crawling. Still at least our streets will be safe for 18 months from the man who wants to spend his life in the gutter. (*The Sun*, 20 April 1993)

There were several reports of sexual attacks, using terms such as 'psychopath' or 'maniac'. The *Daily Star* reported on a rape trial in which:

SEASIDE SEX FIEND GETS FIFTEEN YEARS   (8 April 1993).

After the trial at Preston Crown Court, one of the attacker's victims told the *Daily Star* how he had threatened to kill her if she resisted: 'Do what I say ... I'm your everyday psychopath'.

On 22 April, the press reported that two British tour 'reps' in Greece were raped by a man wielding an axe. The *Daily Star* and *The Sun* led with headlines which labelled the attacker as unstable:

HOL GIRLS RAPED BY AXE MANIAC   (*Daily Star*)

GREEK AXE FIEND RAPES TWO BRIT HOLIDAY REPS   (*The Sun*)

The *Daily Star* goes on to describe the attacker as a 'monster'. However, other versions make no reference to his mental state. If anything, they cast doubt over the truth of the women's accounts of the attack, pointing out that they were either drunk or made conflicting statements to the police. *The Sun* ended its report with a description of the island as an idyllic holiday spot popular with foreign tourists.

The conviction and sentencing of a man for the attempted rape and murder of an old age pensioner was reported in detail on *Scotland Today* (Scottish Television, 23 April 1993), and in the *Herald*, the *Scotsman* and *The Sun* (24 April 1993). They all reported that the man claimed to have heard a voice and seen his elderly victim as his wife. However, only the *Herald* referred to psychiatric evidence from the defence that the man was 'suffering from reactive psychosis and diminished responsibility at the time of the offence'.

Television news and six daily newspapers also reported the sentencing of a student nursery teacher for sexual assaults on 60 children in his care. The story appeared on 21 April on *The Nine O'Clock News* (BBC1) and on *The News At Ten* (ITN), and on 22 April in the press. Television news reported only that the man was sentenced to seven years, with *The Nine O'Clock News* adding that the man warned the children that '... Father Christmas wouldn't visit them if they told anyone'. Press reports focused on the mental state of the attacker and on the physical and psychological damage he inflicted on his victims.

The student nurse, was described variously as a 'sex fiend' (*Daily Star*), 'sex pervert' and 'sex monster' (*Daily Record, Daily Mirror*). The *Daily Sport* labelled him a 'sicko' and a 'sick pervert' whose 'reign of depravity was spread over 10 months'. Three of six newspapers referred to psychological explanations for his behaviour as submitted in his defence at court (*Daily Mirror*, the *Scotsman*, and the *Herald*), as being 'sexually inhibited' and 'the product of "a somewhat chaotic family background"' (the *Scotsman*) during which time he lacked 'a stable father figure' (the *Herald*).

All press accounts included prosecution details of the damage which his victims were suffering. Typical was the *Scotsman* which reported that some children suffered genital damage and long-term behavioural changes. They had 'feelings of anxiety, insecurity, tantrums, aggression and hostility, nightmares about monsters and bedwetting' (24 April 1993).

Stalkers
The most recurrent single theme in Category 2 was that of 'the stalker'. In most press stories (43 items) this is a person who obsessively follows a famous individual such as the fashion model Cindy Crawford:

PSYCHO FAN STALKS CINDY – Pervert kipped in supermodel's bed (*Daily Sport*, 6 April 1993)

CINDY TELLS OF MANIAC WHO LIVED IN HER FLAT (*Daily Mirror*, 6 April 1993),

the rock singer Phil Collins:

MY MAD FAN HELL – Phil Collins tells of woman stalker (*The Sun*, 7 April 1993),

or the Scottish comedy duo, The Krankies:

MAD MIDGET STALKS THE KRANKIES – She threatens to kill Janette (*Daily Record*, 12 April 1993)

SICK MIDGET STALKS KRANKIES' JANETTE – 'Death threats terrify me' (*The Sun*, 12 April 1993)

The 'stalker' often refuses to give up following his or her idol, or sending messages to them. *The Sun* reported the story of a woman who stalked the lead singer of Scottish rock band Deacon Blue:

CRAZED FAN OUT TO KILL DEACON BLUE (*Sun*, 15 April 1993)

The Sun described the stalker as 'a crazed female fan' who claimed she was planning to 'murder the husband-and-wife pop team then commit suicide so "she can marry Ricky in heaven"'. Her obsession was such that she 'gave up her job and sold her flat to track the pair around the country'. This was an unusual stalker story in that some days later, *The Sun* featured a story on the woman, allowing her to explain why she was stalking the Deacon Blue singer:

I'VE SPENT £37,000 AND FIVE YEARS ON MY MASTERPLAN TO WED RICKY – Susan tells of quest for Deacon Blue star (23 April 1993)

The woman was allowed to show how the singer was sending her secret love messages through the words of his songs. She told *The Sun*: 'I am not some crazed fan. All I want to do is meet Ricky and show him my project.'

In two stalker stories, the object of obsession – and violent attack – was an 'ordinary' person:

HOSPITAL STALKER IN SEX ATTACK ON NURSE – Knife is held to her throat   (*Daily Mirror*, 27 April 1993)

TWO DIE IN SIEGE HORROR   (*Daily Star*, 28 April 1993)

The latter item reported how a man killed his estranged wife and then himself. He had already been charged with the attempted murder of his wife but was released on bail. He was reported as having 'stalked' her to her new home.

When the tennis player Monica Seles was stabbed during a match in Germany on 30 April, the incident attracted widespread media coverage. There were 18 items in our sample. Her attacker was described as 'a maniac' (*Daily Mirror*, 1 May 1993), 'crazy fan' (*Daily Record* and *The Sun*, 1 May 1993), a 'nutter' (*Daily Star*, 1 May 1993), and 'a madman' (*Daily Sport*, 1 May 1993). There was some uncertainty at first whether the attack was motivated by political reasons (Seles was Serbian by birth) or carried out by a fan of her main tennis rival, Steffi Graf. *Scotland on Sunday* confirmed that it was the latter, and that the man 'stalked' her for a week before carrying out the attack (2 April 1993).

The Waco siege

On 28 February 1993, the US Federal Bureau of Alcohol, Tobacco and Firearms (BATF) moved in to arrest Vernon Howell, alias David Koresh, the leader of a religious sect, at his base near Waco, Texas. He was wanted for the illegal possession of firearms. However, rather than surrender, he and his followers used their weapons to defend their purpose-built compound, 'Ranch Apocalypse'. Four BATF officers were killed in the exchange before the agency withdrew and laid siege to the compound. The first reports on television news were clear about who was to blame and why:

Newscaster: It began when [federal agents] tried to arrest the leader of a religious cult who thinks he's Jesus Christ.

Reporter: The 77-acre compound is a virtual fortress. Cult members are said to carry weapons in preparation for the end of the world.
(ITN, 12.30, 1 March 1993)

Reporter: The sect has a history of violence ever since ... Howell took control in the 1980s. Howell claims to be Jesus Christ and is rumoured to have 15 wives.
(BBC1, 13.00, 1 March 1993)

In the following weeks, a detailed profile of Koresh and his cult emerged from the intensive media coverage. Significantly, most of the information derived from the FBI, cult 'experts' and disillusioned ex-members of the Branch Davidian sect.

The siege came to a climax on 19 April (during our sample period) with the media coverage generating a large amount of data for our analysis. The Waco story accounts for 157 items in Category 2. For our purposes here, we identified four clear themes: (1) Koresh and his cult (43 items); (2) panic about cults in Britain (31 items); (3) the effect of Koresh's cult on 'innocents', namely the children of cult members and the families and relatives of British members (23 items); and (4) the post-siege public debate and inquests into the FBI operation (60 items). Our main concern is with the first three themes because they best highlight how the profile of Koresh and his cult emerges and feeds into existing public fears. Religious cults and mental illness are most commonly perceived in the public mind as extreme and danger-ous threats from the outside. The fourth theme is of interest where the media refer to Koresh's 'state of mind' when criticising FBI siege tactics.

Koresh and his cult
David Koresh was reported as being the 'deranged' leader of the Branch Davidians, a splinter group from the Seventh Day Adventists (*Daily Record*, 2 April 1993). He was a 'Mad Messiah' who thought he was Jesus Christ (*Daily Mirror*, 21 April 1993). This was evidence enough for many that he was mentally unstable and the President of the USA was widely cited:

Newscaster: The President called [Koresh] dangerous and probably insane.
(ITN, 22.00, 20 April 1993; also the *Herald*, the *Scotsman*, *Daily Star* 21 April 1993)

The cult leader was said to believe only in the literal interpretation of the Bible and to quote liberally from the Book of Apocalypse, a text which is full of cryptic references to the end of the world (Armageddon, The Four Horsemen of the Apocalypse, etc.). To fundamentalist Christian groups, such reading is not unusual. To the secular world, the language can connote 'extremism' and in some cases 'madness'. When the BATF launched another assault on 'Ranch Apocalypse' on 19 April, the compound went up in flames, killing most of the cult members inside. The media adopted biblical imagery to describe the scene:

APOCALYPTIC END TO WACO SIEGE   (*Scotsman*, 20 April 1993)

HELLFIRE   (*Daily Mirror, Daily Star, The Sun*, 20 April 1993)

TORCHED IN THE NAME OF GOD   (*Daily Star*, 20 April 1993)

THE HELL THAT WAS WACO HQ   (*Evening Times*, 20 April 1993)

SUICIDE IN THE FLAMES – 'Sit back and wait until you see God' (*Daily Record*, 20 April 1993)

IT'S SATAN RETURNED TO EARTH – 'The walls were burning, the books were burning, my friends were burning' (*The Sun*, 21 April 1993)

Reporter: Across the still smouldering embers ... a slow search today for what's left of an apocalyptic cult and the 86 people who burned to death for it – a hellish scene illuminated now and then by the sight and sound of exploding ammunition.

A debate followed about whether it was mass murder, mass suicide, or a tragic accident. Whatever their final verdict, the media agreed that ultimate responsibility lay with the 'Mad Messiah', David Koresh:

Reporter: Koresh last week threatened that FBI agents would be consumed by fire if they tried to harm him. Tonight, it looks as if [he] may have turned that fire on his own people.

(BBC1, 21.00, 19 April 1993)

Reporter: Koresh had warned that the 51 day-old siege ... might end in a holocaust. As fire raged through his compound it looked very much as if this was one of [his] prophecies which may have come tragically true.

(ITN, 22.00, 19 April 1993)

It appeared the crazed Koresh was determined his prophecy of an apocalyptic end would come to pass. (*Daily Record*, 20 April 1993)

Crazed cult leader David Koresh always swore he would 'die by the flames of hell' according to a former follower. (*The Sun*, 20 April 1993)

A senior FBI officer said that Koresh 'wanted to have as many people killed ... as possible. That is why it was named "Ranch Apocalypse"' (*Evening Times*, 20 April 1993). As media interest began to wane, the *Herald* was reporting that: 'Public opinion appears to have concluded that the primary responsibility for the deaths of 86 people in the compound ... lies with Koresh' (23 April 1993).

To explain who Koresh was and how he was able to exert such influence over his followers, the media focused on certain aspects of his character that suggested he was unstable. We found one reference to Koresh being clinically ill. The *Daily Star* reported that the cult leader's belief that he was Jesus Christ was an example of 'a bizarre psychological disorder called "Jerusalem Syndrome" where sufferers believe they are the reincarnation of a biblical figure' (20 April 1993). He was also portrayed as having a 'charismatic personality', or 'deadly charisma' (*Herald*, 21 April 1993), as someone who could control and manipulate the minds of his followers to do his will, and as always capable of extreme violence. However, much of this derives from the FBI or from people who met Koresh in Britain and is not based on any clinical analysis.

There was apparently no end to Koresh's powers of control over his followers. A 'cult expert' told the *Herald* how Koresh put recruits through intensive initiation meetings after which they were 'mentally zapped and prepared to take what he said at face value' (20 April 1993). ITN reported that members were 'subjected to the mind-control techniques that are the hall-marks of all dangerous cults' (22.00, 20 April 1993). There was no shortage of testimony from former members:

You don't take anything in anymore. You just sit there like a vegetable. (ITN, 22.00, 20 April 1993)

When I was under David's spell, I would have done anything for him, even die. He would tell us, 'I am God. I can choose when you live or when you die'. (*The Sun*, 21 April 1993)

The sister of one of the members told the BBC that communicating with her brother became more difficult as time passed:

When you spoke to him he was speaking back to you in the words of the Bible, not in normal speech. He was completely brainwashed by it.
(BBC1, 21.00, 20 April 1993)

Stories of sexual abuse of women and children were widely reported in the media. For example, Koresh was thought to have set some of the women aside as his own personal harem supposedly to fulfil a prophecy in the Book of Apocalypse. They were presented in the *Daily Star* as SEX SLAVES OF THE MAD MESSIAH. Koresh was reported to have humiliated them and their male partners to enhance his sense of power and his 'iron grip' as leader (21 April 1993). Most of these stories were given out by the FBI who were routinely quoted as a source. They offered no evidence for their claims but they were reported in most cases as fact.

Koresh's use of doomsday imagery and violent rhetoric was amplified by the media to suggest he was beyond reason and negotiation:

Reporter: Koresh had always maintained he would not leave [the compound] until he had – 'a message from God'.
(BBC1, 21.00, 19 April 1993)

Reporter: Koresh said he was waiting for a message from God before he would surrender.
(*Newsround*, BBC1, 17.00, 20 April 1993)

The Sun carried two items describing the inventory of heavy weaponry which 'gun mad' Koresh had at his disposal. They were headlined:

GOSPEL OF THE AK47 (21 April 1993)

THE DEADLY ARSENAL (22 April 1993)

The reports claimed that the cult leader armed his followers in preparation for Armageddon, the ultimate war between good and evil, and had a special elite force of women called 'the Hellcats'. One item reported an FBI rumour that the women were trained to use babies as shields in a fight to the death (*The Sun*, 22 April 1993).

Koresh was, then, a man who apparently lived and died by the gun:

Cult members have told how Koresh ate his food off a box of live grenades. (*Daily Mirror*, 22 April 1993)

Searchers have found the body of mad messiah David Koresh ... lying on top of a million rounds of ammunition in a concrete bunker. (*The Sun*, 26 April 1993)

Panic about cults

Stories like these fed a panic response about cults and their influence on people's minds. The Waco siege was commented upon by people in our audience study. One person described the fears that these images had raised in her: 'It made me realise how easily people could be coerced into abnormal behaviour and how people could be so totally controlled on such a large scale' (Interview, 14 May 1993).

As the Waco compound was destroyed, politicians called for cults to be banned altogether or at least restricted. Newspaper columns and leader comment prescribed drastic measures and showed little sympathy for the adult victims of the Waco fire. The language they use does not suggest an enlightened response to either religious cults or mental illness:

No one will mourn the death of Koresh and most of his crazy followers. (*Evening News*, 20 April 1993)

SAVE OUR SOULS FROM MANIACS   (*Daily Sport*, 21 April 1993)

CRACKDOWN – It's time for war on the weirdo cults (*Daily Star*, 21 April 1993)

It is doubtful if Koresh, consumed by madness and delusion and hell bent on martyrdom, would have allowed anyone out alive.... You can't negotiate with madmen ... The world is well rid of Koresh and his crazy followers. It means fewer lunatics to warp the minds of others in future. (Richard Littlejohn, *The Sun*, 22 April 1993)

SHOULD WE CURB THE CRAZY CULTS? – You say it's time to stamp out the mad messiahs (*Daily Record*, 24 April 1993)

Apart from the kids, does it really matter how many died in the Waco inferno? The world is full of crazy people. A few less is no great loss. (Frank Fearless, *Daily Sport*, 24 April 1993)

TRAGEDY OF OUR CRAZY WORLD – Waco is a typical example of a modern sickness. The criminals are right and the law enforcers are wrong. Also, those who delude themselves into worshipping and obeying an obvious loony should escape all consequences. (Woodrow Wyatt, *News of the World*, 25 April 1993)

WHY BE SORRY FOR THE WACO LOONIES? – The State can't protect religious loonies who want to kill themselves ... shouldn't the Americans be pleased their society is free of a few more bampots? (Melanie Reid, *Sunday Mail*, 25 April 1993)

A common assumption was that the cult threat came from outside Britain, that 'it could never happen here'. According to the *Daily Star*, 'John Major pledged he will use criminal law to stop evil foreign freaks from recruiting here' (21 April 1993). It was accepted that there are cults in Britain but that, unlike in the United States, they are not so extreme. For example, the *Daily Star* described the leader of the 'British Waco-style cult', the Jesus Army, as 'relatively sane compared with Koresh' (21 April 1993). Some journalists remarked that this situation is helped by Britain's more restrictive gun laws which have so far 'prevented the mad from becoming bad' (Bob Miller, *Sunday Post*, 25 April 1993).

Innocent victims – children in the cult/relatives and friends of cult members
Throughout the siege, the FBI focused media attention on the fate of the children in the compound. They claimed that Koresh was committing systematic child sexual abuse and, as with his subjugation of women, that he cited the Bible as justification. The stories they released were explicit in content and a large section of the media reported them without question. A sample of TV news and press headlines gives an impression of the tone and substance of the reports:

Reporter: The decision to end the siege was taken when it was thought conditions inside the compound were getting worse ... and it was feared that innocent children were suffering.
(*Newsround*, BBC1, 17.00, 20 April 1993)

Reporter: The FBI ... insisted they had to act. Listening devices smuggled into the compound provided further evidence of Koresh abusing young girls trapped inside.
(BBC1, 21.00, 20 April 1993)

SUFFER THE LITTLE CHILDREN   (*Daily Star*, 21 April 1993)

THE CHILDREN WILL BE SAFE IN THE BUNKER – CULT LEADER'S BIGGEST LIE. Devil told cops the kids would be spared then he gave the order to burn them alive. (*Daily Mirror*, 21 April 1993)

DAD LED OWN KIDS TO SLAUGHTER – The last vile act of lying leader Koresh (*The Sun*, 21 April 1993)

'HE SHOT THE SCREAMING CHILDREN ONE BY ONE' – Koresh blasted kids in execution tower (*The Sun*, 23 April 1993)

TOTS FOUND SHOT IN THE WACO RUINS (*Daily Mirror*, 23 April 1993)

Some of the media were more sceptical about FBI claims. Reporters put them in the context of the public row over the tactics employed to break the siege. The most critical of these were from ITN. Bill Neely reported from one of their news conferences at Waco:

These are worried FBI men. They can't explain why they had to assault the compound though they suggest – *offering no evidence* – that children were suffering inside.
(ITN, 22.00, 20 April 1993, our emphasis)

Throughout their coverage, the media focused on the relatives and friends of some of the British cult members killed at Waco. Much of this was in the voyeuristic, 'How do you feel?' school of enquiry. For example, ITN filmed a man watching the compound burn, live on Cable Network News. His whole family was inside and he was in obvious shock, yet the cameras stayed as he tried to reason it all out aloud to himself. The press had a morbid interest in this suffering, too, but a few newspapers reported on how the bereaved families could seek counselling for post-traumatic stress disorder (*Daily Record* and *Daily Mirror* 21 April 1993). The *Evening Times* reported that such treatment was similar to that given to Beirut hostages Terry Waite and John McCarthy (20 April 1993).

Dealing with the 'Mad Messiah': the FBI siege tactics
After the siege, American politicians and other public figures called for an official inquiry into how the FBI handled the siege. While many agreed with President Clinton that the cult leader was 'dangerous and probably insane', more still thought this good reason to have taken a more cautious and patient approach. ITN was particularly critical in this regard:

Newscaster: (LIVE-LINK TO REPORTER AT WACO) We've just heard [the FBI] say the operation was 'carried out with professionalism and care'. Is there any suggestion that they may have got this ever so slightly wrong?

Reporter: It seems ... the FBI misread and miscalculated the actions of this cult at every step of the way and in the end provoked the very action from the cult that they sought to avoid – a mass killing. So there are a lot of questions to be answered.

Newscaster: [TO CAMERA] As we've heard, the FBI's already been criticised for perhaps miscalculating the actions of Koresh and his followers. For 50 days they employed a 'softly, softly' approach. The last time tough tactics were used was on day one ... That resulted in 10 deaths. Tim Ewart reports on how the FBI apparently got it wrong *again* today.
(ITN, 22.00, 19 April 1993, emphasis in original)
The ITN reporter then suggests that the FBI's tactics may have brought the siege to its terrible climax as much as Koresh's mental instability. They tried cutting off communication and power links:

Reporter: Next, psychological warfare – blaring music, probing search-lights. (TANKS ARRIVING ON SCENE) *All the time the build-up of arms continued, leading inexorably to today's confrontation.* (our emphasis)

A 'security psychologist' backed this up with the suggestion that there were other alternatives for dealing with people like Koresh. Some of the newspapers were less restrained in their criticism. The FBI, said *The Sun*, had wielded 'a provocative sledgehammer to crack an unstable nut' (21 April 1993). The *Daily Record* stated that they were almost as mad as Koresh and would have 'a Hell on Earth job explaining their wacko actions' (20 April 1993).

In a later report, ITN cast doubt on the FBI's claim that Koresh had planned to burn the compound down:

Reporter: They have offered no evidence and if they did hear talk of a blaze they did not alert the fire authorities.

(ITN, 22.00, 21 April 1993)

It was later claimed by cult members who had escaped the blaze that it was started by FBI vehicles ramming the compound buildings and knocking over kerosene lanterns. Overall, however, in the media the blame for the tragedy seems to have been laid very largely with the sect itself and the coverage of the events had apparently some impact on public beliefs, both about such religions and on mental 'disorders'.

Additional reports

There were two other major stories which occurred just outside our sample period and which are important to us as they were raised in discussion and interviews with our audience groups for the second report. These were the siege of a Paris nursery school by a man described as mentally ill and the sentencing of the nurse Beverley Allitt, for the murder and grievous bodily harm of children in her care.

Paris nursery school siege
This began early on 13 May. *The Sun* reported that 'a mad masked gun-man' walked into the school as classes began and held a class of nursery school children and their teacher hostage (14 May 1993). In return for their safe release, he demanded £12 million and safe passage away from the scene. The *Daily Mirror* reported that 'police were worried about the mental state of the gun-man ... He had not slept for 36 hours and wept during negotiations' (15 April 1993). By the end of day two of the siege, *The Nine O'Clock News* opened with the headline:

The French gun-man has threatened to bleed his child captives to death but there are signs he may get the ransom he demands.

(BBC1, 21.00, 14 May 1993)

The siege ended nearly 48 hours later, on 15 May, when the police entered the building and shot the man dead. ITN's lunchtime bulletin opened with this summary:

Newscaster: The Paris school siege ended dramatically this morning when French police shot the gun-man dead. The six infants and their teacher being held hostage weren't injured. Police said the gun-man had 16 sticks of dynamite strapped to his belt. The French Interior Minister ... told reporters 'The nightmare is over. The madman has been killed!'.

(ITN, 13.00, 15 May 1993)

BBC News did not quote the Interior Minister's declaration until its late evening bulletin. Its opening summary was almost identical to ITN's:

Newscaster: Six little girls and their teachers are tonight safe and well after police commandos stormed their nursery school ... and ended a two-day siege. They shot dead their captor who had strapped sticks of dynamite to his body. A government minister said, 'The nightmare is over. The madman has been killed!'.

(BBC1, 23.00, 15 May 1993)

BBC News reported that, in the immediate aftermath of the siege, the French police changed their version of what the man's motives had been and the threat he posed to his captives:

Reporter: the police psychiatrist ... told reporters they thought in fact the gun-man had not been after money but was mentally ill and had staged the siege to attract attention to himself. That made him in the eyes of the authorities all the more dangerous.

(BBC1, 13.25, 15 April 1993)

In a later bulletin, a paediatrician who had been allowed in to examine the children described the man as desperate:

Reporter: She said given the chance the gun-man would have detonated the explosives – 'He told me several times he had nothing left to lose in his life'.

(BBC1, 17.50, 15 May 1993)

Beverley Allitt

The nurse, Beverley Allitt, was convicted of a total of 26 charges ranging from murder to grievous bodily harm with intent of children in her care at Grantham and Kesteven Hospital, Lincolnshire. It took a jury six days (12–17 May) to consider the verdicts. Headlines from *The Sun* and the *Daily Mirror* on 18 May 1993 included:

HANG HER – Murdering Nurse Allitt should die say families   (*The Sun*)

HOSPITAL WAS WARNED NURSE WAS MAD BUT DID NOTHING   (*The Sun*)

I SURVIVED ANGEL OF DEATH'S POISON NEEDLE – Boy re-lives killer nurse ordeal   (*Daily Mirror*)

DEADLIER THAN MYRA HINDLEY   (*Daily Mirror*)

HELPLESS YOUNGSTERS WHO WERE VICTIMS OF THE PITILESS 'ANGEL' (*Daily Mirror*)

Afterwards, both the counsel for the prosecution and for the defence told the court that, for the past four years, she had been receiving treatment for a rare mental illness. This led her to inflict injury on herself, and eventually on children, for attention. Media accounts of the proceedings varied in the amount of detail given to her illness. *The Nine O'Clock News* referred to it in its headlines:

After the final guilty verdicts, the court was told that she suffers from a dangerous personality disorder

(BBC1, 21.00, 17 May 1993)

The bulletin reported the symptoms of the illness in detail as described in court:

Reporter: Allitt was suffering from … Munchhausen's Syndrome by proxy [and] had been receiving treatment for … a series of self-inflicted injuries. That … was an earlier form of the illness, Munchhausen's Disease, during which she appeared in casualty frequently with minor injuries to her hands, legs, and back.

(BBC1, 21.00, 18 May 1993)

The Sun reported that Allitt 'had a bizarre mental condition that made her murder for kicks. Allitt was not certifiably insane – but would do anything to get attention for herself' (18 May 1993). The *Daily Mirror* gave a detailed account of the 'early signs of the sickness that would warp her mind' (18 May 1993).

It is clear from the material which we have analysed here that stories linking mental illness with violence have a very high profile in popular media. This is a pattern which is repeated in fictional accounts.

Category 2: violence to others (fictional representations)

In this section, we discuss primarily the content of films, magazines and television drama, including soap operas. For films we analysed the plots of those shown on television in our sample period and reviews of contemporary releases. In films shown on television, Richard Dreyfus pursued a 'crazed killer' in *Stakeout* (ITV, 27 April 1993) and Kurt Russell played a reporter intensely involved with a 'psychotic killer' in *The Mean Season* (BBC1, 30 April 1993). On BBC2, Ronald Coleman played the role of a 'murderously obsessed' actor in *A Double Life* (13 April 1993). Similar themes were referred to in newspaper and magazine reviews. *The Sun* comments on a 'psycho author' and the *Daily Sport* to a 'psycho cannibal'. The *Herald* wrote of plays by 'the New Brutalist School of Writing' which explores 'something nasty creeping out of the woodwork of the deranged characters' collective psyche' (6 April 1993). The men's style magazine *Arena* featured a profile of the actor Dennis Hopper, known for his portrayal of the 'archetypal American psycho in *Blue Velvet*' and who specialises in playing 'psychos, dipsos and weirdos' (Spring 1993).

The teenage magazines in our sample included similar articles. For example, the film review section in *Big* gave the highest rating of '7 out of 10' to a new release, *A Taste of Killing*, in which students are befriended by a 'complete nutter' and 'twisted psychopath' (21 May 1993).

In the period of this sample, none of the 'classics' of the genre (such as *Psycho*) were actually shown though, as our audience study will indicate, such films had clearly made a deep impression on public memories and beliefs. Their success depends in part on people's real fears about their own society and safety in a world which is perceived as dangerous and unfriendly. Such films exploit these fears and intensify them by giving a greatly exaggerated account of the actual risk from 'random maniac killers'. The *Herald* in the period of our sample ran a feature which attempted to explain the attraction of such themes. But in doing so it reinforced exactly this view of potential risk. It quotes Caryn James of the *New York Times* as commenting that: 'It is this element of getting into the mind of a killer while at the same time being safe that lies at the heart of the appeal of books and films about such killers, *especially when we are all potential victims of their random mania*' (13 April 1993, our italics).

Women's magazines/children's fiction

In the women's magazines of our sample, the themes of 'obsession', 'mania' and depression are all developed in fictional stories. *Bella* featured a mini mystery about a woman 'obsessed' who killed out of jealousy (21 April 1993). It also included a story, 'On the Loose' about a 'maniac', who is actually the narrator's ex-husband who has escaped from prison to return to her (14 April 1993). *Woman's Own* had 'Eating Mother', a story which focused on a man's memories of his mother's 'melancholia' which led her to kill his baby brother (28 April 1993).

Adventure strips, cartoons and comics for children were also a source of material linking danger/harm with 'madness'. The comic strip *Batman* appears on children's television in a cartoon version. In one episode Batman's life is taken over by the 'mad hatter'. Batman believes that he is 'losing his mind' and his father suggests that 'you need professional help' (ITV, 09.30, 10 April 1993).

One of the most remarkable growths in children's fiction in the 1990s has been that of computer games magazines for the Sega and Nintendo systems. These are now thought to be read by around 30 per cent of adolescent males (*Guardian*, 6 May 1993). Most of their content is taken up with profiling new games such as *Desert Strike*, which has very obvious parallels with the Gulf War of 1991. The enemy in the game is a Middle Eastern 'nutter':

> You are sent on a series of desperate missions to demolish the evil empire of General Kilbaba, a middle eastern nutter, who's threatening the free world with nuclear Armageddon. In you go, in your Apache Attack helicopter with your chain-gun blazing through mission after mission. (*Sega Power*, June 1993)

Another game celebrates the violent elements of human development through history. Its advertisement runs as follows:

> A *New World* has been formed and on it there are 28 islands. It will take an Eternal God to conquer them all. It will take someone who will lead a team of

men in a *battle* to remove all trace of other life forms from the islands. Someone *skilful* enough to guide those men through the advancing ages of *technology*, from prehistoric times through the middle ages, the Victorian era, the present day and beyond. Someone capable of forming and *breaking* alliances with opposing *forces* without a second thought. Someone to oversee the *construction* of buildings and the mining of materials necessary to build *weapon* designs. Ultimately it will take someone *strong* enough to *fight* for their *divine right* to rule supreme. (*Sega Power*, June 1993, italics in original)

This game is called 'MEGA-LO-MANIA'.

Soap operas

In terms of fictional sources, soap operas are certainly among the most powerful conveyors of meaning, with their huge audiences, which can be as many as 17 million people for a single episode. Most of the main programmes featured characters who were clearly indicated as being mentally ill. *Brookside* on Channel 4 featured the story of Trevor Jordache. Mandy Jordache and her two daughters move into a 'safe house' in Brookside Close. They are in hiding from Trevor who was jailed for violence against his wife. He finds the family, with help from their neighbours who are convinced that he is the charming man he appears. He then persuades his wife that he has changed and she allows him to move into the house until he finds a flat. Popularly referred to by TV critics as 'psycho Trevor' (*Daily Star*, 19 April 1993, *Daily Sport*, 21 April 1993), his portrayal quickly alternates between an amiable loving family man and violence. His *bonhomie* and broad grins to the neighbours accompany dialogue such as: 'Not a bad little club this, is it?' (*Brookside*, 28 April 1993).

But in another scene viewers see this dramatic exchange which begins with Trevor climbing into bed beside his sleeping wife:

Mandy: Get out of here or I'll call the police. Get out of here and leave me alone – leave us all alone.

Trevor: You won't tell anyone because if you do I'll kill you, do you understand? I'll kill you and I'll kill the girls and I'll kill myself. I've got nothing to lose. If I can't have you I'd rather we were all dead. (17 April 1993)

The *Daily Star* commented on this episode, referring to Trevor as a 'passing psychopath' and concluded that 'the sooner his wife and kids butcher the berk the better' (19 April 1993). Trevor's violence does in fact escalate until his wife stabs him fatally, then buries his body in the garden. In our own audience research, one person described how some of her ideas about mental illness had come from seeing Trevor in *Brookside*:

[He] was extremely violent – it was like watching the film *Psycho* – the slightest thing could trigger him off to a violent rage. He had sexually abused both his young girls and was extremely violent to his wife – he ruptured her spleen and burnt all her legs. (Interview, 13 May 1993)

Fictional themes often develop in 'waves' and similar storylines can be reproduced in rapid succession by several media outlets. For example, a successful film may be copied by TV drama, and soap operas will borrow themes from each other. In late 1992, *EastEnders* on BBC 1 introduced a storyline based loosely on the feature film *Fatal Attraction* (Paramount 1987).

In the *EastEnders* version, Michelle Fowler has a one night stand with a student, Jack Woodman. She tells him that she doesn't want a relationship. However, he telephones her constantly, befriends her family, secretly takes photographs of her, resorts to deliberately injuring himself to gain her sympathy and refuses to believe that she is not in love with him. When Michelle's daughter is abducted she wrongly suspects Jack and he responds by making anonymous calls to her. He is clearly labelled as mentally ill, as Michelle says to a friend that 'it's like he's obsessed, it's like he's mad'. He is also referred to as a 'basket case' (15 April 1993) and a 'nutter' (29 April 1993). Michelle's solution is to drive Jack away by using violence. Michelle asks him to dinner and when he arrives he is met by a gang of 'heavies' who drag him outside and beat him up badly. Jack, however, is undeterred and continues calling her. Eventually Michelle arranges to meet his parents to discuss the problem.

The episode broadcast on 29 April is the first to attempt to add some insight to Jack's background and possible reasons for his behaviour. His father reveals that Jack was badly affected by his parent's divorce and asks Michelle not to involve the police. He also reveals that Jack was 'obsessed' with another girl who dropped charges in return for money. Michelle accompanies Jack's father and stepmother to visit him. He reveals how *he* perceives his harassment of Michelle:

Jack: Yeah, maybe you ought to be more careful then shouldn't you? Maybe you ought to *think* before you start trampling over other people's feelings. So maybe you *will* think twice now, uh? People like you and Gina need to be taught a lesson they never forget. Oh yeah, you won't screw me just because of a few harmless phone calls but never *once* do you think about what *you* have done to me!

Jack then asks 'are you planning on having me banged up in some loony bin?'. He becomes more and more distressed as he denies that he will harass Michelle again:

Jack: It's okay, I won't be doing that. I thought she was okay at first but now she just bores me. She's just some brainless stupid bitch, a bit like the one you married. Okay, you want me to come with you? Okay, all right – let's not forget your books, Jack. Don't want you to get behind in your studies, like nice books that are cheap, not twisted boys who get it wrong all the time. Oh, of course and don't forget your clean underwear Jack, well you might get hit by a truck! (*EastEnders* 29 April 1993)

Jack leaves the series after this episode and he is discussed once more when Sharon asks Michelle how the meeting was resolved. Michelle replies 'It turned out that he's a complete headcase' (4 May 1993). Feature items in the press referred to the character as 'psycho student Jack' (*The Sun*, TV Guide, 3–9 April 1993), 'a complete nutter' (*Fastforward*, 10 April 1993), 'psycho Jack' (*The Sun*, 30 April 1993), and 'mad Jack' (*Sunday Sport*, 2 May 1993).

The longest running and most popular British soap opera is *Coronation Street* (Granada TV). From early 1993, it developed a storyline which is important for this study, since we used it in the analyses of audience responses in our second report. The storyline combines elements of the films *Fatal Attraction* (Paramount 1987) and *The Hand that Rocks the Cradle* (Buena Vista/Hollywood Pictures 1991). It begins with the arrival of Carmel, a young Irish woman, who moves in to live with two well-established characters in the story, Gail and her husband Martin Platt. She is there, apparently, to look after their children but several early signs alert viewers to Carmel's obsession with Martin. For example, she is overheard talking as though she was married to Martin and the children were her own. Gail then spends the night away from home and when Martin returns after drinking, Carmel climbs into bed with him. Martin assumes he is in bed with his wife and Carmel later convinces him that they have had sex. When he tries to move her out of the home she assumes it is to a 'love nest' and refuses to believe that he is not in love with her. Carmel then states that she is pregnant by Martin and also attempts to abduct Gail and Martin's child. In a powerful scene Carmel grabs hold of Gail at the top of the stairs as they argue over Martin. Carmel falls and is admitted to hospital where it is discovered that she is not actually pregnant at all. Her grandfather comes from Ireland to take her home and it transpires that Carmel has been 'obsessed' with another married man and that this has happened before.

In the development of this story Carmel is clearly labelled as 'possessed' and mentally ill. Gail discusses her predicament with her friend Alma and states that:

> Her eyes were cold, it was like she was possessed – she means to take Martin away from me … You didn't see her eyes – she says she will stop at nothing and I believe her. (*Coronation Street*, 21 March 1993)

In another scene Carmel confronts Gail after Martin has left his college course to avoid meeting Carmel:

> Carmel: He packed it in? And you'd ruin his career just to get what you want?

> Gail: And what do you want? Apart from a damn good psychiatrist?
> (Reshown, BBC 1 *Going Live*, 3 April 1993)

We spoke with the *Coronation Street* storyline office about the construction of the Carmel story. A member of the production team told us that in researching it they had used an article on erotomania which had originally appeared in *Vanity Fair* in September 1991 (see Chapter 2,

p. 23). There was no other advice sought from outside agencies. The production priorities are clearly towards a powerful and frightening drama rather than how the audience perceived or respond to mental illness. The programme's impact is increased by a very careful use of lighting and scene construction. A key confrontation between Gail and Carmel is lit in shadows, with close-ups to highlight the drama.

The impact is also increased by the specific casting of the Carmel character as a 'fresh-faced home-loving Irish girl', who is then shown to be intensely devious and manipulative. Carmel's own sense of reality is absolute and this is very threatening as she constantly presents the situation as if it is Gail who has the problem rather than her. At one point she even suggests that Gail should see a psychiatrist. It is a measure of the story's impact that it was featured in other programmes such as the BBC's *Going Live!*. In this the actress who plays Gail (Helen Worth) is interviewed. The presenter, Sarah Greene, comments on how frightening it was to watch and Helen Worth replies:

> Helen Worth: I think that was perhaps a lot due to Catherine Cusack who was playing Carmel – a smashing actress, she was just so quiet and so nice all the time.
>
> Sarah Greene: A face of an angel.
>
> Helen Worth: Yes and this underlying terror.
>
> (BBC 1, *Going Live!*, 09.00, 3 April 1993)

This is very much a Hollywood image of madness and horror – the charming stranger who is really homicidal. It also corresponds to popular images of mental illness as the 'split personality'. Such images can be traced through a succession of films and other popular media – for example, a film such as *Three Faces of Eve* (TCF) was a huge box office success in 1957 and started a cycle of films promoting the popular image of schizophrenia. The development of such popular mythologies on mental illness has clearly continued apace in the soap operas. The Carmel story is especially interesting since it had such a powerful impact on audiences. It produced intense emotional responses and antipathy towards the Carmel character, which will be explored further in Chapter 5.

Category 3: violence to self/suicide

Most of the material in this category is from non-fictional sources. We have divided it into four areas: (1) stories which focus on the 'bizarre' nature of self-inflicted injuries or suicides; (2) material which is potentially sympathetic, looking at family or other background circumstances; (3) stories which raise questions about the quality of care in relation to injuries or suicide; (4) discussion of rates or patterns of suicide such as 'copy-cat actions'.

The first area is very much the territory of the tabloid press. There was extensive coverage given to the story of a man who had apparently jumped from the top of a high-rise flat and survived by landing in the middle of someone else's car (*Daily Record, Daily Mirror, Daily Star, Daily Sport*, 3 April 1993). The *Daily Sport* reported a similar case in which a man jumped 50ft from a tower-block only to land in a large dustbin below. The newspaper called it the MIRACLE OF THE BIN AND GONER (6 April 1993).

The newspapers also reported the death of a patient who had knifed himself:

Horrified police looked on as a man stabbed himself through the heart in a busy casualty ward. (*People*, 18 April 1993; also in the *Daily Sport* and *Evening News*, 19 April 1993)

The tabloids also focused on sexual angles which could be linked to suicides as in these examples:

SUICIDE OF SEX SLAVE NUTTER   (*Sunday Sport*, 26 April 1993)

TRAGIC PATIENT HAD SEX FANTASY   (*The Sun*, 20 April 1993)

Suicide is, however, an area which can also generate considerable sympathy in news reports. Thus *The Sun* reported the death of a model with the headline:

DEATH LEAP 'A CRY FOR HELP'   (4 April 1993)

The death of a Conservative Party worker was reported in the *Daily Record* with this headline:

SECRET PAIN OF SUICIDE TORY   (8 April 1993)

On 10 April there were reports of a man who had killed himself because he believed that his mother had rejected him:

A man who tracked down the mother who left him as a baby electrocuted himself because he felt she had rejected him again. (*Daily Mirror*, 10 April 1993)

On 26 April both press and television gave extensive coverage to the death of a father who had killed himself and his daughter after the break-up of his marriage:

A tragic Dad crazed by the break-up of his marriage killed himself and the little daughter he loved. (*Daily Record*, 27 April 1993; also in *Reporting Scotland* 25 April 1993, *Evening News, Herald, The Sun*)

The issue of the adequacy of patient care was raised in reports of the death of a man being treated at Gartnaval Royal Hospital. Both television and the press focused on claims about the 'unlawful' use of electro-convulsive therapy:

A fatal accident inquiry has heard a claim that electro-convulsive therapy was administered unlawfully to a patient at Glasgow's Gartnaval Royal Hospital shortly before he committed suicide. (*Reporting Scotland*, 18.30, 21 April 1993)

The story was extensively covered between 19 and 28 April, including the testimony of the mother who blamed 'neglect' for her son's death:

BEREAVED MOTHER BLAMES HOSPITAL STAFF (*Herald*, 20 April 1993)

SON DIED OF NEGLECT, MOTHER TELLS FATAL ACCIDENT INQUIRY (The *Scotsman*, 20 April 1993)

The *Daily Record* focused on the circumstances of the death as the man jumped from the Erskine Bridge:

VOICES PLAGUED MAN IN DEATH PLUNGE (*Daily Record*, 21 April 1993)

There were also a number of stories at this time about the alleged dangers of television programmes which could induce 'copy-cat suicides'. A letter in the *British Medical Journal* had linked cases of overdosing on paracetamol with a fictional portrayal in the television series *Casualty* (BBC1). The story was then picked up in the *Daily Mirror*, the *Evening Times* and the *Daily Sport* (2 April 1993).

Finally, there were a number of stories on current rates of suicide and attempts by the government and the Samaritans to reduce these. They were given added prominence as stories because the Princess of Wales had apparently been enlisted to help:

CARING DI ON SUICIDE CRUSADE (*The Sun*, 2 April 1993)

The Samaritans campaign focused on the problems of farmers; as reported in the *Scotsman*:

The Samaritans suggested yesterday that there could be one Scots farmer a week committing suicide, wracked by crushing debt and loneliness. (24 April 1993)

We can see from this analysis that while some reports stress the bizarre or violent nature of suicides, others clearly focus on the events as tragedies and explore human backgrounds of depression and anxiety which give context to the actions. This is an area which is also developed in fictional material.

Fictional representations

There were five of these in this category. The medical drama *Casualty* (BBC1 30 April 1993) portrayed an attempted suicide. A woman is admitted to hospital after a motorbike accident. Hospital staff realise that the accident was deliberate when she tells them:

It's all right – you don't have to stay with me. I can't try it on for a bit can I? While there's life there's hope. (*Casualty*, BBC1, 30 April 1993)

All the other items were from a storyline in the soap opera *EastEnders*. The volatile character, Grant Mitchell is to be charged with 'GBH' (grievous bodily harm) and has been waiting trial but he seems increasingly unable to cope with the pressure of prison experience. Other characters express their concern about him saying that, 'if he's in there much longer he'll crack up' and may 'try to top himself' (*EastEnders*, BBC1, 27 April 1993).

The *Evening News* referred to Grant as 'stir crazy' (29 April 1993) and the *Daily Star* described him as 'the human time bomb' (24 April 1993). The actor who plays Grant is quoted as saying, 'Grant is very close to the edge. He could really blow up – or kill himself' (*Daily Star*, 24 March 1993). In the story, Grant has been abusive to his wife and she decides to split up with him. When she visits the prison, however, she is struck by the dramatic change in Grant's attitude as he describes how he feels being on remand:

It isn't *you* stuck in a cell with two blokes. It isn't *you* getting the sweats at night when the cell door shuts – like the walls are closing in on you. (*EastEnders*, BBC1, 29 April 1993, emphasis in original)

Then Grant apologises for his violent behaviour:

I was a bastard to you wasn't I? I can't blame you for wanting rid of me. I had my chance and I messed it up. I always do. I am glad that you came because I wanted to tell you I'm sorry (Grant begins to cry). (*EastEnders*, BBC1, 29 April 1993)

EastEnders clearly used this storyline as an opportunity to depict Grant in a more vulnerable light. Such fictional representations, together with some of the news stories examined above, represent clear attempts at sympathy and understanding towards those involved. We explore this dimension of media coverage further in our next section.

Category 4: Prescriptions for treatment/advice/recovery

Non-fictional material

The great bulk of these items relate to the theme of how to 'cope' with mental illness. There are a very small number of others which offer 'positive' images of mentally ill people showing their ability to recover or live relatively competent/independent lives. We counted 92 items on the theme of how to 'cope' with mental illnesses such as depression (32), schizophrenia (6) and obsession or compulsion (2). There were also items which looked at how people cope with mental illnesses associated with eating disorders (27), sexual relationships (8) and pre-menstrual tension or syndrome (5). Our purpose here is to show how the media deal with problems of mental illness and the solutions they offer. There are four different areas or formats in which solutions are offered – news reports, features, problem pages/phone-ins, and medical/health columns.

News reports

There was extensive reporting of a speech by the Princess of Wales on bulimia nervosa on 27 April. Most items were sympathetic in tone and interpreted the speech as a personal testimony, as much as one made to raise public awareness about bulimia or anorexia. Both press and television recorded long passages of her speech in which she described the symptoms of the disease and the mental illnesses associated with it. The *Evening Times* summarised these in a brief item:

> DI PUTS FOCUS ON EATING – Princess Diana today helped raise awareness of eating disorders with a speech in London. Such disorders include bulimia nervosa, anorexia nervosa [and] food avoidance emotional disorder in which food avoidance is the main symptom. Others include depression and anxiety.

An item in *The Sun* featured criticisms that the speech by the princess was a cynical act of self-publicity in the context of her separation from Prince Charles. The journalist Mary Kenny wrote:

> I'm sure Di is sincere but she is identifying herself with a neurotic affliction which does kill young women – and yet she looks wonderful on it. (29 April 1993)

The *Scotsman* also reported on the inquest into the death of Jennifer Gibbons one of 'the silent twins' once condemned for life to Broadmoor Hospital (23 April 1993). However, the report takes more interest in her life story than in the details of her death. The report begins by relating some of the background to her early life and establishes that she and her sister June were sent to Broadmoor after 'retreating into an impenetrable private world' in which they 'developed an extraordinary relationship verging on psychic'. They were diagnosed as suffering from 'a psychopathic disorder which made them elective mutes' and were 'detained for an indefinite period'. While in Broadmoor they were kept in separate wards. They both attempted suicide and attacked each other on occasion. Eventually a journalist, Marjorie Wallace, met them and established a rapport with them against all expectations. She visited their family home and discovered they were both talented writers. They grew to trust her and then to communicate with her. Soon, they were allowed more freedom and took part in work duties and leisure activities in the hospital. Jennifer Gibbons died of unknown causes.

The debate over 'care in the community' provisions also raised the possibility of discussing the nature of mental illness. However, the reports in our sample on community care all focused on groups such as the elderly or the disabled. For example, BBC News concluded that:

Community care for the old, the mentally and physically disabled was introduced with almost universal approval ... but many councils around the
country now fear it may lead to more neglect of the frail.

(BBC1, 21.00, 1 April 1993)

There was one report on BBC Scotland from just before our sample
period, which did look specifically at provision for people who had
mainly suffered from schizophrenia. It is notable in that the journalist
consciously presents a sympathetic image of people helping themselves. It is also critical of state provision in the area. We interviewed the
Home Affairs Correspondent for BBC Scotland, and he made these
comments about his report:

We filmed in a half-way home and in Gartnaval Hospital. The suggestion was
that the provision wasn't going to be sufficient. In the half-way house ... there
were people who were mainly schizophrenic and they seemed to be quite at
home where they were. One [shot] was of a lad making himself a meal and
frying himself a bit of bread. This was showing how it could work – but there
wasn't enough money to get all of the people out of the state institutions.
(Interview, 1 June 1993)

Such positive images occur very rarely in the media. We found none
in our sample period but include two further items from outside the
period to show some alternative portrayals.

Scotland Today (Scottish Television) featured an item on care in the
community which included the image of a woman living alone in her
own home in Shotts, near Glasgow. She was 51 years old and was
reported to have lived in a number of institutions for most of her life.
The item shows her making herself a cup of tea and settling down to tell
the reporter how she is coping with her new situation:

Woman: I've never looked back. I've enjoyed every minute of it and I still
enjoy it. (*Scotland Today*, 31 March 1993)

There is one other report which is of interest here in that it raised
critical questions about the nature of social responses to mental illness. Three Scottish newspapers reported on an industrial tribunal
hearing on the unfair dismissal of a nurse from her post at a psychiatric hospital in Paisley. She was sacked for holding what the *Herald*
described as an 'underwear party' for her patients. The tribunal
awarded her substantial compensation and ordered the hospital to
reinstate her. The *Herald* reported the findings of the tribunal, including the observation that the patients 'seemed to have enjoyed themselves at the party'. This was despite the claims by the hospital
authorities that '[the nurse's] behaviour had been inappropriate and
below the standards expected' (24 April 1993). One of the key points
was that only women patients were present and that only underwear
was shown for sale. The tribunal's findings implicitly raised the issue
that if 'normal' people can attend parties for the sale of underwear
then why can't the patients of such an institution. But the raising of

such issues in media accounts is extremely rare and the sense of the mentally ill as being harmful and potentially dangerous is pervasive. This, of course, has been one of the features of the community care debate, with a persistent trickle of news reports on local opposition to the siting of new facilities in communities. (*Scotsman, Evening News,* 14 April 1993).

Feature journalism
Most feature journalism in the sample was confined to single items on depression, compulsion, and illnesses associated with eating disorders or personal relationships. For example, *Best* devoted a one-page item to questioning whether the local GP has time to deal with problems such as depression (29 April 1993). There was one example of an in-depth enquiry into serious mental illness. The *Evening News* ran a three-part series of full-page feature articles on schizophrenia from 14–16 April. In part one, 'Voices from Within', the journalist Nicola Barry interviewed a patient. By telling his story, she debunked some of the social myths about the illness:

> Everybody has heard of schizophrenia but few people know what it is. Jokes are constantly made about split personalities or Jekyll and Hyde characters. People make the mistake of thinking the illness is a split between good and evil.... One in a hundred people suffers from schizophrenia. It fills more hospital beds than any other disease. Yet still it is a taboo subject ... 'the secret illness'. (14 April 1993)

In part two, 'Agony in the Home', the journalist examined the impact schizophrenia has on the ability of the schizophrenic to cope with life, and on his or her relationships with family and friends (15 April 1993). Part three was entitled 'The Door To Nowhere', and assessed the quality of care and support available to sufferers. (16 April 1993)

Problem pages
In problem pages or TV phone-ins, readers or viewers spoke about having a mental illness or knowing someone who has. They describe the problems the illness creates in their lives and how they try to cope with them. In some cases, they also ask for advice or help. Here are two examples from the problem pages:

> I was depressed and even thought of taking my life. I telephoned the Samaritans all the time. ('Dear Deidre', *The Sun*, 26 April 1993)

> I'm neurotic. I don't know what's wrong with me. I'm depressed a lot of the time ... and feel lonely and unhappy. Can you help me please? ('Kit Dallas', *Evening News*, 23 April 1993)

The conventional response for the 'agony aunts' or 'uncles' is to offer sympathy, and readers are normally referred to psychotherapists or specialist counsellors.

Medical pages and health columns

Medical or health columns by doctors or psychotherapists are more likely to offer detailed explanations for a particular illness. For example, *Woman* magazine of 12 April 1993 devoted their 'Case Book' feature to the subject of depression. This included news and information, self-help tips, a personal testimony by someone who had suffered serious depression, and an item by 'Dr Alan'. The doctor begins by making a distinction between common sense notions of depression and a medical diagnosis before going into detail about the symptoms of the illness and the problems it creates:

> What doctors call depression, or rather depressive illness, is more than simply feeling down in the dumps ... In most cases of true depression ... day-to-day functioning can be affected so that the sufferer can't carry on. (*Woman*, 12 April 1993)

This type of format is also more likely to deal with those types of mental illnesses which are least understood in the public mind. In a letter to Anne Hooper of *Best* magazine (29 April 1993), a reader tells how she has been diagnosed as schizophrenic:

> Reader: But no one has ever explained to me what the causes are and what effect it's likely to have on my family ... What can I do?

> Hooper: Nobody fully understands what causes schizophrenia – experts can't decide if it's due to a stressful childhood (as indeed yours was) or to a chemical imbalance in the brain. Either way the result is the same: there are times when you will feel depressed, paranoid or irrational and may even start to hear voices ... However, experts agree on one thing: if you've been prescribed medication, it's vital that you take it regularly. This will control the symptoms and reduce stress on you and your family.

In two items from our sample, the professional advocated more openness about mental illness and stated that people can cope and recover. Tom Crabtree ('On the Couch') is *Cosmopolitan's* resident psychotherapist. He usually deals with a single reader's problem in detail. In the magazine's May issue, he reproduces a letter from someone who suffered from 'a nervous breakdown' and has recovered:

> Reader: The details of my recovery might sound very promising, but can you tell me why mental illness is still a taboo subject in our society?

> Crabtree: Mental illness is taboo because it's scary. People are frightened of things they don't understand. These days, we know a lot more about mental illnesses, but there are certain forms that we can only control and hope that the patient will get better. This isn't as bad as it sounds. Using new drugs in combination with sensitive treatment, we can now tackle virtually every form of mental illness. Most people who become mentally ill get better. (*Cosmopolitan*, May 1993)

In a letter to 'Dr Mike' of *Woman's Own*, a reader wants to know if the term 'nervous disorder' is a tactful way of saying 'nervous breakdown'?

77

The doctor makes a clear distinction between 'neurological disorders' and 'nervous breakdowns':

> However, these days there should be less need to be tactful about describing a mental breakdown. In the majority of cases, there's no known reason why it has arisen and, in any case, it's not a sign of weakness as was once thought. (*Woman's Own*, 28 April 1993)

This letter was very clearly in the direction of redefining attitudes.

Fictional material

A common theme in all these items was that the conditions portrayed were unthreatening and non-violent. For example, the hospital drama *Casualty* (BBC1) contained two storylines, one about a patient with Munchhausen's Syndrome and another about a member of staff whose mother has Alzheimer's disease. The patient with Munchhausen's Syndrome talks about the origins of her condition saying:

> When I were 18 I collapsed one day when I were out shopping ... [it was] me appendix. I came to and everyone were fussing round me – ambulance men, nurses. I had three weeks of it. I'd never felt like that before. I belonged. (*Casualty*, BBC1, 23 April 1993)

The nurse suggests that she talks to someone about it. The patient replies:

> Patient: You mean a shrink?

> Nurse: Well, why not? It's just an illness like any other, isn't it?

In another *Casualty* episode, Norma, the hospital receptionist, is worried when a junior doctor jokes that she may have inherited Alzheimer's disease from her mother. She is reassured by the head nurse who says:

> Think about it. When has Rob (junior doctor) ever set eyes on your mother? As for you, the reason you've been forgetting things is because you have a lot on your mind. (*Casualty*, BBC1, 30 April 1993)

The nurse later complains to the consultant about the junior doctor's behaviour.

The children's drama *The Lowdown* produced 'An Open Mind' (BBC1, 4 May 1993), which reconstructed a fictional case of child therapy. Produced with programme consultants from the Child Psychotherapy Trust, this programme was reassuring and sympathetic. The child's teacher tells his mother:

> Lots of kids have problems. Growing up is a difficult business and some of them sometimes need help with it. If Jack had a bad knee I'm sure the doctor would have a look at it. It's the same with emotional problems.

The drama gives the address of the Child Psychotherapy Trust in the closing credits.

Other sympathetic portrayals were carried in the hospital soap *Medics* (ITV 26 April 1993) in which 'Professor Hoyt' is depicted as withdrawn and remote after his wife dies. The *Daily Star's* preview of the programme commented that:

> On the surface it seems that he is coping with the death of his wife by throwing himself into his work, [but] it looks increasingly likely that he cannot save himself from his anguish. ('Today's Choice', *Daily Star*, 26 April 1993)

The soap opera *Brookside* also introduced a storyline about depression with the character, Deborah 'DD' Dixon. Although she was previously portrayed as tearful and uninterested in life, the first real indication that she may not just be low after the 'flu is when her husband calls out the family doctor. He recommends a week's course of anti-depressants and asks about their marriage; her husband is having a secret affair (*Brookside*, 26 April 1993).

In such portrayals of depression, the characters can appear as helpless victims in deep anguish. They may then produce rapid recoveries as the exigencies of the plot dictate. In *Coronation Street*, the character Emily Bishop is almost blasé about her own illness shown in earlier episodes. In this exchange, the character Vera Duckworth proposes that Emily use her illness to get them both off a court fine:

> I think if you tell them you've had an attack of your old problem – you know you went mental. Well I mean you did go in that psychiatric hospital didn't you? You tell them that they're bound to be sympathetic.

Emily replies:

> I am not going to pretend to be mentally deranged in order to get myself off a motoring offence! (*Coronation Street*, ITV, 21 April 1993)

The fact that Emily is a popular character, and that she can cope with talking about her illness in this way, does indicate the possibilities for a more sympathetic and positive coverage.

Category 5: critical representations

We found little in news reports or from other factual sources which could be classified in this way. The definitive fictional account in this area is *One Flew Over the Cuckoo's Nest* (novel by Ken Kesey 1962, film 1975 UA/Fantasy) which questioned how mental illness was defined and contrasted the 'community' of the patients with the institutional violence to which they were subjected. The film was not shown in our sample period but it was referred to several times by members of audience groups when discussing the formation and development of their own beliefs. There was very little of any similar material in our sample, but one episode of the drama *Casualty* (BBC1) did explore critical issues in the social definition of behaviour as 'irrational' or 'unbalanced'. The plot focuses on a woman admitted to hospital after an accident. It transpires that she has attempted to murder a man by shooting him with a crossbow and he has also been admitted to the same hospital. The nursing staff begin to realise that she is responsible:

Nurse: Where did you have treatment?

Patient: What do you want? Psychiatrist, psychologist, psycho-therapist, counsellor? Look at my notes! My problem's unbalanced, deliberately prolonged grief, grief process hampered by deep-seated sense of injustice. Can't be relied upon to take her medications, wants to face up – can't face up.

She explains that eight years ago her daughter was killed by a drunk driver. He was never prosecuted due to the influence of his father, Lord Bradbrooke. She continues by saying: 'Not any more though, his poncey father can't fiddle things for him now.'

The nurse informs the police that the patient was responsible and she is to be charged with attempted murder. Other hospital staff, however, question the decision to disclose this information and also challenge the idea that her actions were criminal or 'unbalanced':

Consultant: Are the police still with that poor woman?

Nursing Sister: Do you know what? I think if I'd been Charlie, I'd have kept my mouth shut. I mean if somebody killed Laura and I woke up every morning knowing that he got away with it ...

Consultant: Well don't worry, he'll die of cirrhosis of the liver by the time he's 40.

This item is not typical and indeed it is very unusual to find material which goes beyond the normal boundaries of 'sympathy'. Most material which is intentionally sympathetic confines itself to examining the tragic circumstances surrounding depression or anxiety and to expressing general fears about the adequacy of care or financial provision. Even these items are in a very clear minority. As we have seen, the bulk of media content situates mental illness in a context of violence or harm and presents the public as 'potential victims of random mania' (*Herald*, 13 April 1993).

Such representations can clearly affect audiences. They can alter perceptions of the 'dangerous' nature of mental illness as well as affecting beliefs about the risks of random attacks by the 'maniacs' who are presented as populating the world. We have also seen how fictional products can be structured to generate very powerful responses of hatred or dislike towards central characters who are portrayed as mentally ill. The media do have an important role in the development of beliefs about mental illness and in the generation of such affective responses. The next chapter uses audience groups to explore these issues in greater depth.

CHAPTER 5

The media and public belief

Greg Philo

This chapter links the examination of audience beliefs with the analysis of media content which we have given above. Here, we will trace the processes by which key messages are received, and focus specifically on the conditions under which they are believed, rejected or reinterpreted. We will examine the role of key variables such as personal experience or cultural history and show how these can condition different responses among a variety of audience groups.

Sample

This consisted of six focus groups with an average of 10 people in each, drawn mainly from the west of Scotland. The groups were structured to be broadly representative of income levels, occupation and housing type for this area. Such a sample is not large enough to make generalisations about the whole population. Its function was to examine the processes by which beliefs and attitudes develop. As such, the groups did generate an extraordinary range of data. Their precise composition is as follows:

> **Group 1, Lenzie (14 May 1993)** This is a commuter suburb, north of Glasgow. There were 13 people in the group living in owner-occupied housing, mainly in lower middle-class occupations such as secretaries, computer operatives, a building society worker, a beautician, together with housewives and older children who were still at school.

> **Group 2, Mossend (19 May 1993)** This is a working-class area of Lanarkshire, situated next to the Ravenscraig Steel Works. There were 11 people in the group, living in council housing. Most were unemployed or working in part-time unskilled occupations together with one skilled template maker, a pub manager and a hairdresser (see Fig. 5.1).

Group 3, Glasgow West End (20 May 1993) This group of 11 people represented the social mix of Glasgow's west end, an area which combines expensive owner-occupier property with rented accommodation for students and lower income groups. Typical occupations of its members were shop managers and shop workers, pharmacy, nursing and unemployed ex-students.

Group 4, Motherwell (26 May 1993) This was a group of 11 people predominantly from skilled working-class occupations: self-employed slaters, joiners, electricians (for the males) and shop assistants or clerks for the females (see Fig. 5.3 and 5.4).

Group 5, Milngavie (1 June 1993) This is a middle-class suburb north of Glasgow with expensive owner-occupied housing. There were 11 people in the group who worked in the senior management of companies or the local authority plus one senior police officer and an assistant matron of a private hospital, together with the older children of group members who were at private schools or just about to enter university (see Fig. 5.2).

Group 6, Glasgow Hillhead (11 June 1993) This was a group of seven public sector (education) workers of relatively low income, employed as cleaners/janitors, mostly living in rented/council accommodation.

The above six groups constitute our 'general sample', all of which were randomly chosen. Most of this sample was drawn from specific residential areas and there was some effort made to keep its members in what are termed 'naturally occurring units'. For example, such a unit could be a family or couples from particular blocks of housing. Another might be a group of people who all worked together (as in Group 6). These are the sorts of units in which people might meet, discuss, read newspapers or watch television programmes. Such a sampling method gives a wide age range with a relatively even gender balance, while preserving elements of the social culture within which people actually receive media messages.

Methodology

The methods used here for analysing reception processes involve new techniques which have been developed in the Media Group over the last six years. Each session with a focus group is divided into three specific phases. In the first, the group is sub-divided into smaller units of two or three people. These work on exercises which consist of writing a news report or the dialogue for a fictional programme (such as a soap opera). The main purpose of this is to test people's expectations of what they will see in the media as well as their understanding and memory of particular types of media output. The exercises also have the very important function of facilitating a collective activity in which people can begin to express their own ideas in a relatively informal way. While in these groups, people will often discuss the subject matter with the banter and humour that might characterise other social situations such as being at work together. It is very important to produce such 'natural' responses. We have found such a context can help to produce the open expression of views. In the second phase, each member of the group answers a series of questions which focus on beliefs about mental illness and the sources of such beliefs. In the third phase each person is interviewed in depth about his or her own answers. The first two elements of these techniques generate a great deal of data, but it is also possible that some group members may not wish to divulge sensitive information in a group context. In practice we found that the individual interviews were very useful in gathering further information about personal experience, viewing/ reading habits and other specific influences on beliefs and attitudes.

Results – the media exercises (first phase of group work)

This part of the group session involves a series of exercises. In the first, group members are given a newspaper headline and are then asked to write the news story which accompanies it. In the sheet on which they work, the original story has been removed, and they write their own

Figure 5.1   Group 2, Mossend (19 May 1993).

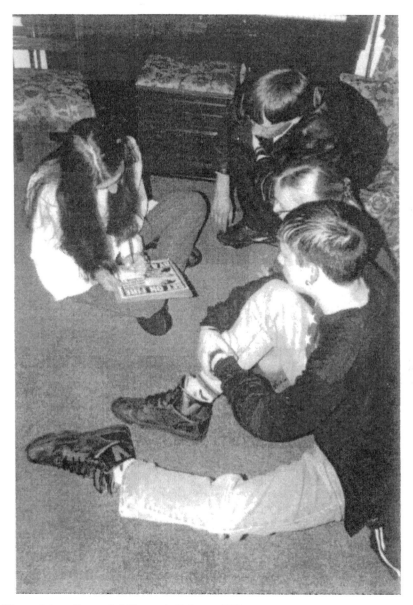

Figure 5.2   Group 5, Milngavie (1 June 1993).

story in the space which this leaves. The headline is about an alleged attack on a young boy in a park. It reads:

SET ON FIRE BY A MANIAC   (*Daily Mirror*, 15 April 1993, see Appendix 2)

The 'attack' was recorded on radio news and in the press. These accounts were actually untrue, as the boys had made up the story and later the newspapers carried disclaimers to this effect. The main purpose of the exercise was to assess the familiarity of the audience with the everyday language and assumptions of the media in stories which accompany such headlines. But it was also interesting to see how many people had picked up on the fact that the story was not true.

In the next exercise, the groups were given a different news headline relating to a former patient in Lennoxcastle Hospital, who had now received a Diploma in Education:

WILLIAM LEARNS TO BEAT THE ODDS   (*Evening Times*, 14 May 1993, see Appendix 2)

He had also been chosen as one of the top five adult learners in Scotland. News reports which stressed positive achievements in such a context were extremely rare in our sample. This one actually appeared on the day of our first group meeting. We decided to include it as an exercise in subsequent meetings as we thought it useful to broaden the range of material on which the groups could work at writing their own stories.

The third exercise was drawn from the soap opera *Coronation Street*. It was based on the story of Carmel, the Irish nurse who has an obsessive attraction for the character Martin. This situation produces a series of confrontations between Carmel and Gail, Martin's wife. The details of this story are given in Chapter 4. In this exercise, the groups were given photographs of characters and scenes from the programme and asked to write the storyline and dialogue. Later, in this second phase of the meeting, the group members were asked a specific question about how they would have reacted in the situations which they have described. The minority of people who had not watched *Coronation Street* were given a different exercise to do, based again on writing a news story. This was on the theme of a 'stalker' pursuing a star:

PSYCHO FAN STALKS CINDY   (*Daily Sport*, 6 April 1993, see Appendix 2)

There was a run of such stories in the period of our study and we deal with them in detail in Chapter 4.

Writing the news

The story of the attack on two young boys is an interesting example of how a completely false account can enter into the 'public store' of memories and beliefs. In our sample, 18 people stated that they remembered the original story of the young boy being set on fire. But only nine of these knew that the report had been retracted and the boys had made up the story about a 'maniac'. It is interesting that the children chose this particular social stereotype for their cover story, after they had started the fire themselves. The description which they gave of their 'attacker' parallels exactly the demonology of popular media. A detective is quoted as saying: 'We are looking for some sort of lunatic', and the *Daily Mirror* tells us: 'He was grabbed by the scar-faced brute' (16 April 1993).

Our audience groups could reproduce the phrasing of the tabloids with apparent ease. The *Daily Mirror* for example, reported that:

> The horrifying attack left 7-year-old Derek Kripps blackened and burned. (16 April 1993)

By comparison, the stories written by the groups used the phrases 'brutally and cruelly attacked' (Lenzie Group), 'horrific ordeal' (Milngavie Group), 'horrific arson attack' (Mossend Group), 'savage attack', 'sickening attack', 'atrocious attack' (Motherwell Group). The attacker was also 'thought to be disturbed and dangerous' (West End Group). The Hillhead Group asked in its story: 'What kind of beast would carry out such an atrocity on a helpless 7-year-old child?'

The fears which such a report can generate are also made quite clear in stories by the groups:

> The incident has caused widespread fear amongst local parents who are reluctant to let their children out of sight. (Milngavie Group)

The following story was written by three middle-aged women from Mossend, who obviously agreed with the sentiments which it expresses. As they were voiced in the group, there was much nodding of heads:

> Police are today looking for the evil maniac who tried to disfigure this innocent child. What kind of world do we live in when a child can't even be allowed to play in the street. (See Appendix 2 for this and further examples)

Figure 5.3 Group 4, Motherwell (26 May 1993).

We live in an environment which is saturated in media products, but it is still extraordinary to see how effortlessly group members can reproduce the different styles of our media culture. This account has the flavour of a *Crimewatch* announcement:

> Police are looking for any witnesses who have seen him in the park at 2.30 p.m. yesterday to come forward. Contact any police office. (Hillhead Group)

These abilities to reproduce the style and content of media accounts were also shown in other exercises. Some members of the groups wrote a news story for the headline: PSYCHO FAN STALKS CINDY. The actual story in the *Daily Sport* ran as follows:

> Stunning supermodel Cindy Crawford has revealed how a prowler broke into her flat ... before she married heart-throb actor Richard Gere ... *the sicko was finally caught after a chilling night-time phone call.* (6 April 1993, emphasis in original)

Five weeks later, three women in the Lenzie group produced this story:

> Stunning model Cindy Crawford, married to Hollywood superstar Richard Gere, revealed at a press conference today that she had been the victim of a crazed psychopath ... The besotted fan had been pestering Cindy with obscene phonecalls over recent months. (Lenzie Group, 14 May 1993)

Two men in the Milngavie group wrote their story as follows:

> Super model Cindy Crawford, wife of Hollywood star Richard Gere has revealed that for the past three months she has been living in fear of attack by an obsessed fan who has been making terrifying threats.

This story is interesting since it also makes the link with the film *Psycho*:

> The fan who identifies with Norman Bates in Alfred Hitchcock's box office smash hit *Psycho* has been writing and telephoning Cindy as well as sending her bizarre and frightening packages. (Milngavie Group, 1 June 1993)

The themes of 'nightmare', 'misery' and 'living hell' run through the group's stories. Thus we have 'a maniac who had been making her life a living hell' (Milngavie Group), and 'who has made her life a misery' (West End Group). Then comes relief after 'many months of anguish':

> Super model Cindy Crawford, the beautiful wife of film star Richard Gere, was last night relieved when police ended many months of anguish. (West End Group)

The 'nightmare' theme occurs in this story:

> Super model, Cindy, revealed to us today the nightmare she has been living for the past two months. (Lenzie Group)

The *Daily Sport* ended its story with the words:

He was jailed for the break-ins and Cindy's nightmare was over. (6 April 1993)

William learns to beat the odds

A very different note is sounded by the report of William Whyte, who had spent 33 years in Lennoxcastle Hospital before receiving his Diploma in Education. The institution is actually for people with learning disabilities, rather than those traditionally defined as 'mentally ill' (though in popular conceptions these tend to be confused). The stories written by our groups reflected the more upbeat content of the news report, and some of the group's 'news' once again came close to actual news reporting. For example, the *Evening Times* story quotes an education official as saying 'William is a worthy winner' (14 May 1993). The West End group produced this quote:

The principle of the college described William as an 'eager learner'. So well done Willie! (See Appendix 2 for this and other examples)

Other stories written by these groups stressed the themes of 'achievement' and 'example to others'. But some developed other themes on 'mental illness' and current government policies such as the development of community care. These stories clearly related to other accounts in the media such as television documentaries on the 'illegitimate' placement of people in institutions. In the Milngavie group, one person cited a specific programme which showed 'how people were put in institutions for what would now be very minor things, like having a baby or dyslexia'. This theme appeared in several stories:

Mr White, 68, was committed to the hospital after being diagnosed as dyslexic as a child. (West End Group)

William was probably admitted to this mental home and probably wasn't mentally ill – and he was just a victim of circumstances. (Mossend Group)

Other stories saw William Whyte's achievement as a possible example of the 'success' of community care policy. This policy had received extensive media coverage, as we indicated in our first report on news content. But much of the coverage had been critical, which is reflected in this rather double-edged commentary, written in the Milngavie group:

The policy of releasing long-term patients into the community has in this case proved to be a positive step in the right direction.

But one has to question if this is an exception to the general policy which has met with criticism from many quarters.

The original story in the *Evening Times* did not contain these themes and indeed William Whyte had left Lennoxcastle Hospital well before the current debate on community care. But the themes are clearly drawn from other media accounts and are then related by audience group members to this story. These are interesting examples of how the media can provide the information for some key elements of public understanding on specific issues. News stories can then be absorbed and perhaps re-interpreted within this context of pre-existing belief and understanding. News reports and 'factual' programmes are only one part of the development of such social consciousness, but they do appear to have a significant influence.

Coronation Street

This exercise produced a quite dramatic response from many people in the groups. As soon as the pictures were shown, there were murmurs of recognition. The animosity towards the character of 'Carmel' was apparent. As the exercise started, there were sometimes comments such as 'She was a bad bitch, wasn't she? She was a swine' (Hillhead Group).

Group members also showed a remarkable ability to reproduce dialogue from the story. For example, in one dramatic scene Sally, the childminder, is looking after Gail and Martin's son, David. Carmel arrives and fabricates a story in order to take the child away.

The scene below was very popular with the groups, perhaps because it ends with Carmel being put out of the house by Sally, who then slams and locks the door. This is the dialogue of the actual scene:

(CARMEL ARRIVES AT THE HOUSE)

Sally: Hello.
Carmel: Hello Sally, ehm, Gail's asked me to do her a favour – ah, hello David, you have got a treat in store, you've been invited to a party.
Sally: David has?
Carmel: Yeah, I've just called into the cafe and one of David's friends mothers phoned Gail – could he go to a party this afternoon – so anyway that's the message and Gail asked me to drop him off, 'cause it's on the way back to college so would you mind getting his coat, I'm in a bit of a hurry. (TO DAVID) You are going to a party – yes you are.
Sally: What friend?
Carmel: Stephen – he sometimes goes round to Gail's. (TO DAVID) You know Stephen, don't you? Yes, of course you do.
Sally: I'll just give her a ring.
Carmel: Why? D'you not believe me?
Sally: I'm not saying that.
Carmel: Well what are you saying?
Sally: I've got to make sure.
Carmel: So you don't believe me, you think I'm a liar, is that it?
Sally: You don't mind if I phone Gail, do you?
Carmel: Course not, why should I? Go ahead. (TO DAVID) Isn't she silly, isn't she?

Sally: Let me have him.

Carmel: Ach, he's all right with me. (TO DAVID) Aren't you?

Sally: While I make that phone call.

Carmel: I'm not doing any harm.

Sally: I didn't say you were. Just give him to me.

Carmel: Why should you look after him? I can look after him as well as you can. (TO DAVID) Can't I? Yeah, course I can.

Sally: Give him to me Carmel before I fetch the police.

Carmel: Oh God, you are so smug. Go on! Phone the police! Phone Gail! No one ever believes a word I say, no one.

Sally: Give him to me please . . . and *get out!* (SALLY SLAMS THE DOOR ON CARMEL AND LOCKS IT)

(*Coronation Street*, 21 March 1993)

On 14 May, seven weeks later, a group in Lenzie produced this version of the scene:

Carmel: Hi Sally, I've just come from the cafe. Gail asked if I would pick David up and take him to a birthday party.

Sally: Whose party? Gail never said anything about a party to me!

Carmel: Remember Stephen from Rosamund Street, David knows him from play group.

Sally: I don't know Carmel – Gail left him with me and I am sure she didn't mention a party.

Carmel: She forgot to tell you. I said I would come and get him.

Sally: Wait a minute and I'll phone Gail.

Carmel: Are you calling me a liar!

Sally: No, but you must realise I am responsible for David and I can't hand him over without checking.

Carmel: Well I'll hold him while you phone.

Sally: No Carmel, leave him! ... Get out, get out of my house! Or I'll call the police.

(Lenzie Group, 14 May 1993)

A group in Motherwell wrote:

Carmel: Gail sent me round to collect David.

Sally: Well Gail never mentioned it to me.

Carmel: I guess she must have forgot because she asked me to pick David up as it would save her some time.

Sally: I will ring up the shop and verify it.

Carmel: Why do you want to ring her up for, do you not believe me?

Sally: But I'm responsible for David and I'm not giving the boy to you.

Carmel: (GETTING VERY CROSS SHE TRIES TO GRAB DAVID BUT SALLY PULLS HIM BACK AND THREATENS HER WITH THE POLICE)

(Motherwell Group, 26 May 1993)

In this exercise the groups were given no information at all about the plot and had to work purely from photographs. Some were extremely accurate in their reproduction of dialogue and in general they showed great competence in reproducing themes from the story line. The key moment in this scene is when Carmel is put out of the house by Sally. It recurs frequently in the material written by the groups: 'Give me the baby back and get out of this house' (Mossend Group), 'Now leave this house before I call the police' (Mossend Group). The Hillhead group put in stage directions for Sally: 'Turns round and bangs door behind her.'

We have already shown in our content study how Carmel was presented as mentally ill and portrayed as something of a demonic character – 'the face of an angel and underlying terror', as one member of the cast had described it (see Chapter 4). The manner in which key scenes were shot also added to the portrayal, being lit with deep shadows, with highlights on Carmel's wild face and glittering teeth. Some group members commented on these shots as they were doing the exercise. In the West End group one woman made several direct references to a picture of Carmel and Gail as being 'eerie' and 'frightening'. Each time she held the photo up for the others to look at and received their general agreement. In the Milngavie group, one member commented 'that's quite scary – her face, her teeth' and another person replied 'she was quite evil-looking in that'.

The Carmel story was remarkable for the intense animosity which it apparently generated among its audience groups. In the second phase of the group sessions, one of the questions which people were asked was: 'How would you have reacted in the situation with Carmel, if you had been Gail?' Two-thirds of the respondents in our general sample gave responses which suggested aggression or violence. These were their replies:

1 Killed her (Male, Hillhead);
2 Battered her bloody mouth in (Male, Hillhead);
3 Kicked hell out of her (Female, Hillhead);
4 Scratched her eyes out (Female, Hillhead);
5 I would have killed the cow (Female, Hillhead);
6 I would probably have reacted very violently or abusively and thrown her out of the house (Female, Milngavie);
7 I would have been very upset and taken violent action and chucked Carmel out of the house (Female, Milngavie);
8 Hit her one (Female, Milngavie);
9 Reported her and forcibly ejected her from the house (Male, Milngavie);
10 Thrown her out immediately (Female, Milngavie);
11 Slapped her and called police and doctor (Male, Motherwell);
12 I'd have been very angry and upset and threw her out of the house straight away (Female, Motherwell);
13 Given her a belt in the mouth (Male, Motherwell);
14 Thrown her out (Male, West End);
15 Violently – she threatened my security and family! (Male, Lenzie);
16 I would have felt the urge to hurt her (Female, Lenzie);
17 I would have sent her packing (Female, Lenzie);
18 I would have been stronger in getting rid of her (Female, Lenzie);

19 Put her out of the house (Female, Mossend);
20 Told her to go and probably hit her (Female, Mossend);
21 I would have told her where to go (Female, Mossend);
22 Slapped her, phoned the police (Male, Mossend);
23 More violent (Male, Mossend);
24 Would react angrily – might become violent (Male, Mossend);
25 I'd have punched her f---ing face in (Male, Mossend);
26 I'd plant one on her chin (Male, Mossend);
27 I would probably have assaulted her (Male, Mossend);
28 I would kill her (Female, Mossend).

There were nine replies which were more sympathetic and which suggested getting medical help:

29 I would have reported her first to the police and then taken her to the doctors for serious and immediate medical help (Female, Motherwell);
30 Angry, but I hope I would have realised as time went on that Carmel was mentally ill (Female, Motherwell);
31 Got a doctor for her (Male, Motherwell);
32 Sent Carmel to see a psychiatrist (Female, West End);
33 Thrown her out of the house, denounced her in public and, with Martin by my side, let the whole world know what she was up to. Then suggested to her that she seek psychiatric help (Female, West End);
34 Involved agency: psychiatry/police (Male, West End);
35 She was unstable and needed some kind of help (Female, West End);
36 I would have realised she had a mental problem (Female, Lenzie);
37 I would have realised that she was in need of help (Female, Lenzie).

There were a further five responses which were non-committal or relatively passive such as 'can't predict' (Female, West End) or 'think out the situation' (Male, Motherwell). There are some apparent differences in the responses between groups. Middle-class groups tended to have more non-watchers of the programme. In the first list of comments, from those who watched the programme, the language of working-class groups was often overtly violent. Middle-class aggressive responses were couched more politely as in 'forcibly ejected her from the house' (Response 9). In the West End group, the middle-class respondents produced a high proportion of sympathetic and non-aggressive responses. But some of these differences clearly relate to the experience of mental illness, rather than to class variables. One member of the West End group was a psychiatric nurse. His response, and that of his wife who was also in the group, clearly reflected this work experience: 'Involved agency, psychiatry/police' and 'seek psychiatric help' (Responses 33 and 34). In the Motherwell group the three respondents who suggested involving doctors or medical help all had very close contact with people who were mentally ill (e.g. their mother or sister).

Figure 5.4 Group 4, Motherwell (26 May 1993).

But experience and overt sympathy towards the mentally ill did not always produce a sympathetic response to Carmel. The story clearly touched very deep nerves in the audience. For example, one member of the Lenzie group expressed great sympathy towards the mentally ill and was very critical of the media for 'always portraying the monster aspect'. He wrote that 'just because somebody has difficulties or deficiencies in certain areas should not detract from their individuality'. But he would have reacted to Carmel 'Violently – she threatened my security and family!' (Response 15). There were other examples of ambivalence towards Carmel. In the list of sympathetic reactions above, one of the suggestions about psychiatric help follows a long agenda of other things which are to be done to Carmel, including being thrown out of the house and denounced to the world (Response 33). The formation of such responses is dependent on a number of complex influences. The issue of how inputs from media can interrelate with direct experience and other cultural factors is crucial, and is a major focus of the following sections.

The questions and interviews

These are the second and third phases of the group sessions. The questions followed on immediately from the media exercises and group members wrote their own answers. In the third phase, each person was seen individually to discuss and clarify their own answers. The questions were as follows:

1 Who remembers the first news story? (If so, write 'Yes I remember it.' If not, write 'No I don't'.) If you remember it, did you know what really happened in the park that day?
2 When I say the words 'mentally ill', what comes to your mind? What are the first things that come into your head – words, phrases, pictures, someone, or what?
3 What is a mentally ill person like – what symptoms might they have, how might they behave, what would you expect a mentally ill person to be like – how would they act – how would you recognise them as being mentally ill?
4 What informed your answers to questions 2 and 3 – where did your ideas on this come from – was it direct knowledge, someone you have known – or something you have read in papers or seen on television, something people have said. Where did the ideas come from?
5 Think about media reports or stories on serious mental illness – I'm thinking of people who might be referred to as 'mad', 'psychotic', 'schizophrenic'. Would you say that these people were mostly associated with violence or would they not be, in media reports and stories?
6 Do *you* associate such mental illness, what might be described as 'schizophrenia'/'psychosis' with violence? Would you say people who are 'schizophrenic'/'psychotic' would be quite likely to be violent or quite likely not to be violent?
7 What informed your answer to question 6?
8 Think about TV and press coverage; and stories about people who are mentally ill. Has anything that you have seen or read changed what you thought about mentally ill people – made you more afraid or less afraid – more or less sympathetic, or less worried, more worried? If so, can you say what it was that affected you – and what the change was?
9 *Coronation Street* watchers – how would you have reacted if you had been Gail – what would you have done in the situation with Carmel?

In this series of questions, the first and the ninth relate to the media exercises and the responses to them have already been dealt with above. The purpose of questions 2, 3 and 4 was to give some indication of sources of beliefs about mental illness. In practice, they were very important questions as they did show the extent to which people based their views on direct experience. For example, some people gave very accurate descriptions of particular illnesses, based on work experience or describing members of their own families. The remaining questions focus on how mental illness is understood and specifically on its associations with violence. We have already seen in our content analysis how such a focus is established in media accounts. Question 5 takes up the issue of what people believe the content of media to be. Questions 6, 7 and 8 explore the issue of how such content might relate to the development of belief.

The media and belief

The responses given to the original questions and those from the interviews did show that media output can influence some key elements of beliefs about mental illness. One of the key issues explored here was whether serious mental illness was associated with violence and whether people with illnesses such as schizophrenia were 'quite likely to be violent'. Forty per cent of the people in the general sample believed this to be so and gave the media as the source of their belief. Beliefs about schizophrenia were related by group members to images from both factual and non-factual sources. This description from a woman in Motherwell combines both of these:

> A lot of things you read in the papers and they've been diagnosed as being schizophrenic. These murderers – say that Donald Neilson, was he no' schizophrenic? – the Yorkshire Ripper ... in *Brookside* that man who is the child-abuser and the wife-beater – he looks like schizophrenic – he's like a split personality, like two different people. First he gets like self-pity and he brings flowers and works his way back into the house and you could feel sorry for him, then he's a child-abuser and a wife-beater. (Motherwell Group, Interview)

Another person developed a similar theme based on the film *Fatal Attraction*:

> They could be all right one minute and then just snap – I'm kind of wary of them ... that *Fatal Attraction* she was as nice as nine pence and then ... (Interview, Mossend)

Such comments can reveal very deep levels of fear. One woman in Lenzie wrote in her replies that mentally ill people were 'quite likely to be violent – split personality usually tend to be violent'. She went on to write that, 'I would tend to be more wary as some mentally ill people can be very clever and devious'. The source of her views was given as 'probably from TV and newspapers, I think!' and she went on in her interview to comment that:

> Hungerford, that type of thing – anything you see on the news, it's likely to be violent when it is connected with mentally ill people. (Lenzie Group)

The amount of media coverage linking mental illness with violence was referred to by several people in the groups: 'Almost every programme you see about mental illness ends with violence in some form or other' (Milngavie Group); 'Any programme I have ever seen of mental illness had violence in it' (Hillhead Group). Both of these people cited media content as the source of their own beliefs. Most members of the groups believed that the featuring of mental illness in the media was dominated by images of violence (although not everyone accepted these images as being accurate).

We have shown in our study of media content that such images of violence do predominate in both fictional and non-fictional media output. The responses given in our group studies show how these two sources can inter-relate in the development of belief. For example, a person's understanding of a news report can be developed using elements derived from fictional sources. The Lenzie group was interviewed on the day that the nurse Beverley Allitt was found guilty of the murder of children in her care. One young woman in this group described the news story in terms derived from Hollywood horror:

> The nurse who killed the babies – you know, you could imagine a smile on her face as she was doing it – injecting them.

Some film images clearly had a major impact on members of the groups. Films such as *Silence Of The Lambs, Psycho,* and *Halloween* were frequently referred to. People spoke of being really shocked by some moments in films and it is clear that there was some impact on attitudes towards the mentally ill. A woman described seeing a film about the Kray twins:

> I always thought mentally ill people would not be able to do much for themselves and would be looked after by someone, but then you get evil people like the Kray twins who were evil, violent men who I suppose must have had some form of mental illness to do the things they have done to other people and seemed to enjoy it ... I seen the film – they looked like pretty normal people but they weren't. (West End Group)

The last comment clearly recalls the 'face of an angel and underlying terror' theme which we saw in the Carmel story from *Coronation Street*. In another case a woman spoke of how very frightened she had been by scenes in the film *Death Wish*: 'It scared and shocked me, I avoid films like that now.' She related her own beliefs about violence and the mentally ill to 'Hollywood, film, television drama'. These beliefs had also apparently heightened her anxieties about policies such as community care:

> I feel that government policies in Britain of putting mentally ill people into the 'care of the community' is dangerous. I am sympathetic to the plight of the mentally ill but because they can not get on GP's registers they can't have prescriptions filled. I feel without drugs they can become more of a danger, and I feel more afraid. (Lenzie Group)

These examples give some indication of the influence which the media can have on the development of beliefs and attitudes. But there was another group of people in the sample who were very critical of the dominant message on mental illness.

Rejection and criticism of media images

Some members of the groups expressed a profound distrust of the media, especially of news reporting, which they saw as focusing on extreme cases. A middle-aged man from the Milngavie group questioned the link between mental illness and violence simply on these grounds. He was so distrustful of the media that he in effect believed the opposite of the main trends in reporting. He wrote that his views 'largely reflect media influences', but only in the sense that he did not believe what was being said.

However, most of the people who did not accept the dominant media account of image of mental illness and violence made their judgement on the basis of direct experience. In the general sample, 37 per cent of the group members cited work or personal experience, or knowledge derived from the experience of friends or family, as the key factor informing their beliefs. Two people had worked as nurses with psychiatric patients. One of these wrote of mental illness getting 'a bad press' and of 'sensationalism' in reporting (West End Group). At this time we also interviewed a group of users of mental health services, who were working on a training programme at the Scottish Association for Mental Health in Edinburgh. The members of this group were very critical of the tendency in the media to link mental illness and violence. They cited their own experience and that of meeting many other people who had illness such as schizophrenia. One person wrote explaining why he did not associate such illness with violence:

Some of my answers came from being depressed myself and through this the people I came into contact with gave me more knowledge ... As a day patient, out-patient, occupational therapy ... I met about five people who had schizophrenia.

Another member of the group summarised many of their views when she wrote:

Media headlines regarding mentally ill people, I think create fear through general descriptions of mental illness. The mentally ill are generally portrayed as violent psychopaths and the lack of basic understanding in the general public causes the fear to be multiplied. (Edinburgh Group)

There is, however, an important qualification to be made of such a view. It is certainly true that the media can misinform its audience, but it is also true that the prevalence of mental illness in our society means that many people will have some direct experience through family members or close friends. The members of our groups often cited such contacts as a source of their own knowledge. They were sometimes used to comment on specific news stories. For example, one woman commented on the Beverley Allitt case and used her experience with her mother-in-law to suggest that such violence was not typical behaviour for the mentally ill:

My mother-in-law, she was mentally ill but she wouldn't have done anything like that ... She just seemed to go into a wee world of her own – sort of unpredictable. (Mossend Group)

In another group, a woman spoke of her sister and a friend who were manic depressive. She contrasted her own views with those of people with whom she worked:

> I keep an open mind and I don't believe everything I read. I work with people and I hear what they say but I think they don't really know until they've experienced it. (Motherwell Group)

She also had no time for films such as *Halloween*: 'The likes of *Halloween* and that, I'll not watch them ... just rubbish.' She had, however, watched the film, *One Flew Over the Cuckoo's Nest*, which had greatly impressed her:

> One film stays clear in my mind, *One Flew Over the Cuckoo's Nest*. I laughed all the way through it and yet at the end of the film I felt sad and quite gutted.

This raises the important issue of people's choice of films, television programmes and other media, and how such choices relate both to experience and attitudes.

Experience, choice and 'reinforcement'

Many of the people who had experience of mental illness, and who did not accept the dominant media view, chose to watch minority programmes such as documentaries which treated the issue sympathetically. Such programmes were then cited by these group members as having heightened or developed their awareness or sympathy towards the problems of mentally ill people. For example, one member of the West End group related his own beliefs to the fact that his father had suffered from manic depression and to his own experience of periods of depression. He described a television documentary and the impact which it had made upon him:

> The documentary in which an ITV reporter posed as a schizophrenic in order to highlight the uncaring system which fails to look after them ... He couldn't even get arrested by shouting at people and he ended up sleeping on the streets ... I realised how it was probably easy for society to forget about them and how government policies didn't represent these people. (West End Group)

There was also a smaller number of people in this sample (16 per cent) who had experience of mental illness and who gave this as a reason for associating it with violence. One woman in the Mossend group spoke of living with the violence of her mentally ill husband. As she said, 'I lived with it', and the effect of what she saw in the media was to make her 'more afraid'. In such a case, a violent media portrayal could be seen by her as confirming her own experience. But for some of the others who spoke of negative experiences with mentally ill people, the contact had been more slight. For example, one woman gave an account of seeing someone once when 'on holiday and became a bit wary of them'

(Hillhead Group). A young man described an experience as a child when he had seen an elderly person 'acting crazy' (Mossend Group).

Such experience could then be 'confirmed' or developed by negative media coverage. But it would be wrong to understand the role of the media as being simply to reinforce previously held views. There is more than one message in the media's output and audience responses can be very complex. In this sample, 24 per cent of the group members spoke of being made both more fearful *and* more sympathetic towards the mentally ill by what they had seen in the media. Sometimes this could be from a *single* media product such as the film *Silence of the Lambs*. The man who described his experience as a child (above) gave this account of watching the film:

> (It was) about a middle-aged man brutally killing people, cooking parts of victims' body and eating them, also used parts for furniture. Made me feel sick, sympathetic and afraid towards mentally ill person in film.

Even where people clearly chose a specific 'type' of media output, their choice did not necessarily correspond with their experience. For example, a member of the West End group who would be described as liberal and progressive in his general outlook, chose to read 'the quality press'. Yet part of his experience related to a friend who is mentally ill and who had wrecked his flat and 'assaulted people'. This had resulted in some ambivalence in the attitude of the group member:

> I'm well aware it's not a typical case from what I read in the quality press – but I'm pretty much undecided. (West End Group)

We can see that the relationship between different media messages, our beliefs, social cultures and personal experience is extremely complex. It is not surprising that audience understanding is sometimes contradictory and ambivalent.

Active audience theory

One of our main interests has been to identify what people believe and understand from media messages and how their beliefs relate to other sources of information. In this sense we are interested in tracing sources of belief and affective responses. But there is another group of theorists in this area who focus on the active use by the audience of the television message. They are interested in how audience members develop interpretations, establish the meaning of what they see and how they use television programmes in discussion. Thus James Lull has argued:

> Television viewing is constructed by family members; it doesn't just happen. Viewers not only make their own interpretations of shows, they also construct the situations in which viewing takes place and the ways in which acts of viewing, and programme content, are put to use. (Lull 1988:17)

Lull's work has influenced other theorists, such as David Morley. In a commentary on Lull, Morley notes that:

People often use television programmes and characters as references known in common, in order to clarify issues that they discuss. Television examples are used both by children and adults to explain things to each other – to give the examples and instances which will illustrate the point that someone is trying to make. (Morley 1986:32)

Television viewing is thus very much seen as a communal activity. As Morley writes:

Television viewing is of course something which in many families is precisely done together. In this case the medium can be used to provide opportunities for family members or friends communally to experience entertainment or informational programmes. (Morley 1986:33)

The locus of research for Morley is the family and one of his concerns is with how programme preferences relate to neighbourhood and domestic life. He records his subjects' 'use' of a particular programme and how it becomes the basis for discussion. He describes how the mother of one family relates to *Coronation Street*:

This strong sense of connection between their concrete experience of neighbourhood and domestic life and their programme preferences is well expressed in their mother's comments on the way in which she talks about the fictional series which she watches with her women friends. 'I go around my mate's and she'll say, "Did you watch *Coronation Street* last night? What about so and so?" and we'll sit there discussing it.' (Morley 1986:85)

The emphasis in this work is on the use made of television programmes and the collective discussion of meaning. This emphasis is reflected in and is in some senses achieved by the investigative framework which is employed. A primary interest in such a theoretical approach is to ask audiences how they use TV. There has been criticism of some work in this area on the grounds that the issue of the impact of media on audiences is ruled out by the nature of the theoretical approach. Thus Robert Kubey has criticised the work of Elihu Katz for ignoring the possibility of media effects. As Kubey writes:

Katz and some of his colleagues … focus on television viewing, often giving subjects specific programmes to view, and then the researchers probe these subjects for their interpretations. Most problematic is that Katz explicitly states that 'What interests us, however, is not what people take from television but what they put into it' (Liebs and Katz 1990, p. 5). In deliberately ignoring the entire aspect of media effects and in intentionally choosing only to look for particular phenomena, Katz guarantees that he will find what he's looking for. (Kubey 1996:14)

Our focus differs from that of the active audience theorists in that we begin by establishing the nature of audience beliefs and affective responses and then attempt to analyse the origins of these. One factor which emerges from this approach is that close family groups may have varying beliefs on a specific issue and not be aware of it, since the subject is not discussed.

For example, in the audience study for this volume, we analysed the responses of five family members (two parents and their three children) on the issue of the association of mental illness with violence. This family had been included in our general sample of audience groups. In their case we found that the family members drew their information from different sources. The mother worked as an assistant matron in a hospital and had direct experience of psychiatric patients. She rejected the view that people who were mentally ill would be quite likely to be violent and cited her own experience as the source of her belief. The father (her husband) was a senior police officer and did associate mental illness with violence. He wrote:

(They are) likely to *be* violent. I associate the illness with violence from practical experience. (1 June 1993)

He then commented that: 'We have had two or three murderers who are complete schizophrenics.'

All three children associated mental illness with violence and all cited the media (press, television and films) as their source. As one daughter (aged 17) wrote:

Yes, I would say that people that have a mental illness would be violent. I have this idea as I have seen films about people with mental illnesses being murderers or violent. In newspapers it is always referred to a 'psycho' killing someone.

The second daughter (aged 13) also wrote that:

I say that mentally ill people are in general quite likely to be violent. I got my ideas from television or newspaper reports as I have not seen any mentally ill people in real life.

The son (aged 18) wrote that:

I would think that the majority of people with these sorts of mental illness will be associated with violence.

and commented that: 'All these films like Psycho and stuff like that, you always hear about these serial killers and that and they say that he had a mental illness.'

What is remarkable about these accounts is that none of the family members were apparently aware of the differences in beliefs between them or the differences in the sources of their understanding. The children had their own televisions which they could watch, separately from their parents. More importantly, the issue of mental illness and violence was simply never discussed, as the son commented when asked about this: 'It is not the sort of thing we would discuss really – I can't think we've ever discussed it.'

This was confirmed by a statement from the mother on whether they would talk about an issue such as schizophrenia and violence. She commented that they had 'never discussed mental illness in the family ... It's a no-no area in a family if it doesn't affect you.' This remark raises another very important issue – that the stigma of mental illness to which the media contribute actually pre-empts rational discussion at an everyday level. As the mother remarked: 'There's still a great stigma attached to mental illness – if it doesn't affect people, they don't want to know about it.'

There are important methodological issues raised by the fact that this family did not discuss the area because it was seen as taboo. This may well apply to other 'sensitive' areas such as child abuse, AIDS, alcoholism or sexuality. This raises questions about theoretical approaches which assume that families 'use' television, and methodologies which pursue their data by asking interviewees about the conversation and inter-change which exists within the family. There are two specific problems with such methodologies. First, they focus on 'use' and neglect issues of the impact of messages and the possibility of measuring changes in belief. Second, the methodologies can by definition rule out areas where there is no interchange of ideas or discussion within the family or group. Our research shows clearly that the media can have a powerful impact and that this can sometimes be in areas which are not discussed at all.

Ambivalence, contradiction: conclusion

The media can exert great influence over audiences, but people are not simply blank slates on which its messages are written. The acceptance, rejection or interpretation of the message are all cultural acts. The media exist within developing social cultures: they do not create the whole social world or how we think about it, but they are clearly very important sources of information and can generate strong emotional responses in their viewers and readers. They do so by exploiting key elements of social cultures which they have in part created. For example, some messages on violence and mental illness are located within, and exploit, deep anxieties about security, the unknown and the unpredict-able, in what is seen as a very frightening world. At the same time other images can relate to and develop cultural senses of community, care and concern for people who are seen as helpless, stigmatised victims. It is quite possible for both of these cultural elements to co-exist in people's consciousness.

But such is the depth of anxiety in this area that some media accounts can exert great power. Our research in other areas has found that personal experience was a much stronger influence on belief than media content. One of the most interesting findings of this research is that we found cases where this pattern was reversed. For example, a woman in the Hillhead group had visited Lennoxcastle many times to see a relative who had been a patient there for 25 years. She associated mental illness with violence and cited 'TV films' as the source of her belief. She also gave a list of the films: *'Texas Chain-Saw Massacre, Freddy's Revenge, Nightmare on Elm Street, Psycho* – I watch a lot of them, I like all they ones.' She was asked specifically if the feeling about violence came from the films rather than what she had seen in Lennoxcastle. She replied:

> Oh aye – every time I was up visiting, I never saw any violence and he was in a big open ward. (Hillhead Group)

Sometimes, as we have seen, such personal experience led people to criticise media content. But there were 13 cases (21 per cent of the general sample) where people had non-violent experience which was apparently 'overlaid' by media influences. These people traced their beliefs mostly to violent portrayals in fiction or to news reporting. A further example of this was given by a young woman in the Lenzie group who lived near Woodilee Hospital. She wrote that she had worked there at a jumble sale and mixed with patients. Yet she associated mental illness with violence and wrote of 'split/double personalities, one side violent'. She then went on to say:

> The actual people I met weren't violent – that I think they are violent, that comes from television, from plays and things. That's the strange thing – the people were mainly geriatric – it wasn't the people you hear of on television. Not all of them were old, some of them were younger. None of them were violent – but I remember being scared of them, because it was a mental hospital – it's not a very good attitude to have but it is the way things come across on TV, and films – you know, mental axe murderers and plays and things – the people I met weren't like that, but that is what I associate them with. (Lenzie Group)

In this study, we have seen how the media are part of a very complex cultural nexus. We have shown how messages can structure understanding, how they can be discounted by 'positive' experience in some cases but in other examples how reactions, even to fictional portrayals, can overwhelm experience. In these relationships we can see the media as a crucial variable, not merely for reinforcement, but as a powerful influence in the development of beliefs, attitudes and emotional response in this key area of social life.

CHAPTER 6

Users of services, carers and families

Greg Philo

This chapter examines the possible impact of media output on users of services, their carers, families and others who are close to them. Some mental health professionals have argued that stigmatising media images have a profoundly negative effect on the family relationships and other social networks of those who are mentally distressed. There have been urgent calls for media representations of mental illness to be examined (Atkinson 1994, Hyler *et al*. 1991). Birch (1991) has written of how stigmatising media images can inform a circle of negative responses, both in users of services and in those who care for them. Media coverage of schizophrenia functions to 'pathologise the whole experience of the sufferer' and such coverage 'instructs sufferers, their professional attendants, and their families, in a restricted set of responses to the illness' (1991:22–23)

Liz Sayce, Policy Director of MIND, has also written critically of media coverage which equates having a mental illness with being a highly dangerous criminal. As she notes, there are literally millions of people with psychiatric problems each year but only a tiny number are involved in the acts of violence which feature in media coverage. She comments on the impact of the climate of fear and suspicion on users of services:

> While some users respond with strength, mutual support and humour – 'I've got my axe in my handbag' – the reality for some can be a crushing sense of difficulty in being accepted as potential employees, work mates or friends; and in some cases a collapse in self-confidence. (Sayce 1995b:132)

Organisations such as MIND and Survivors Speak Out, as well as the Royal College of Psychiatrists, are extremely critical of media images in this area. But as yet there has been very little evidence published on the impact of television and press coverage.

Sample and methods

Our own study explores these issues through a series of interviews with users of services. Some interviews were in drop-in centres, where helpers and organisers sometimes sat in on the discussions. Normally these were conducted collectively with groups of approximately six people and these could then be followed up with individual interviews. The purpose was to give people the security of being in a group so that they would not feel pressured to speak. Points that were made in these discussions could then be followed up with direct contacts after the meeting. We interviewed 32 people at drop-in centres and user groups in Glasgow, Manchester, Aberdeen and Edinburgh. In Manchester, the group were users of services who had formed the Schizophrenia Media Agency with the specific intention of challenging media images in this area. We also interviewed a further group of seven people who were working in a training/computer skills programme based at the Scottish Association for Mental Health in Edinburgh. We also spoke extensively with mental health professionals and other workers from organisations such as the Royal College of Psychiatrists, MIND and Survivors Speak Out.

The questions which we pursued focused on public attitudes to mental illness and the sources of information which underpinned people's beliefs and emotional responses. In the interviews with users of services we were interested in what their beliefs had been before they were themselves mentally distressed and how these beliefs had perhaps changed. We also asked questions on the attitudes of carers, neighbours and on work relationships. These specific questions were asked in the group interviews, and formed the basis for discussion:

1 What were your beliefs about mental illness before you became distressed yourself?
2 How did you think of yourself when you were distressed or when/if you were 'diagnosed'?
3 What was the source of your beliefs about mental illness?
4 How did neighbours/family/people at work react?

We should note here the difficulty of gathering data in this area. We have spoken with mental health professionals but they are, of course, governed by codes of confidentiality, so it is not possible to recount individual cases in detail. We have interviewed users of services on the basis that they are willing to take part in the study. But we have to recognise that it is potentially very difficult to ask people to give details of their lives and the reactions of others to them at times when they were in great personal distress. For reasons of confidentiality we have not in most cases identified the place or date of interviews. We have also not tabulated results as might be done in other areas of research such as on beliefs about political parties or voting intentions. This is partly because the sample size is small but mainly because of the intrinsic difficulty of the area, in which people may not speak because of potential distress, rather than because a phenomenon does not exist. However, the purpose of this work is to illustrate, where possible, the processes by which people come to understand and think about themselves and whether these processes can be affected by media output. In this sense, understanding the qualitative nature of these relationships and establishing what does and can occur is more important here than estimating the exact frequency of occurrences within a given group. The people in our groups made clear their view that they saw media representations as a central problem, but it is obviously easier for them to describe this in general terms rather than to recount in detail the impact that stigmatising images have had on their own lives. Nonetheless, some members of these groups did feel able to speak about their personal histories and their testimony is a powerful indication of the impact of media in this area.

Media and public belief

The members of our interview groups overwhelmingly saw television and the press as having an impact in defining public understanding of mental illness. No one suggested that the effect of media was minimal or non-existent in the society as a whole. Some group members also pointed to other sources of influence which had affected their own beliefs, such as direct experience of peer group cultures. But their belief in the power of the media to form opinion was frequently expressed. As one member of the Manchester group commented:

> You are constantly getting bombarded by images that have nothing to do with the illness at all and just reinforce these negative images that are around and ... the whole field of mental illness is being discussed in a climate of ignorance and fear.

A member of the group in Aberdeen commented on the public image of schizophrenia:

> If you said to somebody that I'm schizophrenic, I think their first image would be some mad axe murderer rather than someone who is trying to cope with an illness.

A group member in Edinburgh discussed the difficulty of watching television with his child when it so consistently featured phrases about being 'crazy' or 'a nutter':

> Something that occupies my thoughts is sitting down with my child in front of the telly and the number of images that are about being crazy and a nutter on children's TV, and *Loony Tunes* has a regular slot. It may sound harmless but when almost every other phrase they use is to be 'crazy' or a 'nutter', whether it is the presenter or the characters in the films, I wonder what happens to children when they grow up and have these images put into them.

It was not just popular television or the tabloid press which drew criticism. As another member of a group in Edinburgh commented:

One of the things I really object to is by people who should know better, the chattering classes on Radio Four. [A journalist] will sit in *Woman's Hour*, flinging around the word schizophrenia, you know just completely inappropriately. There were some people doing Shakespeare and they were all playing different parts and she said 'Doesn't that make you feel schizophrenic?' It is basically meaningless and demeaning a very difficult condition that a lot of people have to live with.

This raises the crucial issue of whether media images have an effect on how users of services think of themselves or on their family or other relationships.

Users, carers, neighbours, work

Many professionals in the area of mental health have commented on the power of the media to set agendas for public debate. Helen Storey, the information team leader at MIND, told us that media coverage affects directly the number of enquiries that the organisation receives on specific issues:

We get a lot of these calls after television programmes. You get a television programme about community care and a lot of people will phone up asking about it. We get a direct correlation between the subjects of television and people ringing up. Last week there was a programme about sexual abuse in psychiatric hospitals and we had a lot of calls about abuse – a lot more than usual.

We also raised this issue with organisers and workers at a drop-in centre for users of services. One organiser told us how the assumed link between violence and mental illness affected enquiries which they received:

I had one woman asking me if (she) was safe living in (her) own house 'Am I going to get my throat cut?' She said she loved her son ... but she was terrified, she wanted to know if her daughter would be safe. Her son was on medication and he was due to come home. He had no history of violence ... and this is common.

Liz Sayce of MIND spoke to us of the calls which they receive on the same issue: 'We have had people on our information line saying that I'm worried that my son is going to be violent because it's part of the illness isn't it? – even though he has never shown any signs of violence.'

Liz Sayce quotes a mother writing in the *Guardian* about her daughter, diagnosed psychotic:

Though she has never shown any violent tendencies, how can we be sure what might happen? In the back of my mind is the fear that one day she might harm someone physically. (Quoted in Sayce 1995:30)

However, media images and public misconceptions about mental distress can be challenged by direct experience. One carer described to us how her original views on mental illness changed because she refused to relate them to her own son:

> I was working in a hostel with homeless and people would point at someone and say 'he's schizo', and then I'd read something in the papers or see something on telly – that someone had killed someone, or walked into a lion's den – also in the movies, you'd see someone who was wearing 10 different dresses and had 10 different personalities and they were supposed to be schizophrenic. And then I found out that schizophrenia wasn't split personality and that's only because of my son ... I was full of guilt and anger. I had to start learning because it was my son.

Media images may influence users of services as well as carers and family. As one member of the Manchester group commented:

> I had the same misconceptions as everyone else, split personality, Jekyll and Hyde, flying off the handle at a second's notice, unpredictable aggressive. (These came) partly from the family and possibly from what I'd seen on TV, radio, newspapers ... and when you think, my Dad's read probably two newspapers a year and watched every news bulletin on telly for the last 40 years that's a lot of horror going into one mind.

There are a number of ways in which beliefs derive from media and affect users. One of the issues raised with us by psychiatrists such as Anthony Clare is the potential impact on willingness to seek help. One group member described to us the confusion and fear which he felt when he was first asked to sign himself in voluntarily to hospital:

> I was what's called psychotic, a very distressed state, but I remember thinking, will I ever work again? The prejudice that I carried with me about sufferers of mental illness, I wouldn't get another job – also fear of the institution I was in as well ... images like *One Flew Over the Cuckoo's Nest*, getting dragged off for ECT, all these fears that I would be dragged off for electric shocks once I'd committed myself to the hospital.

Another group member described how she was afraid to go for appointments because of what she had seen in a television drama:

> I'd been quite ill at the beginning of the eighties and I was referred to the clinic and I wc ildn't go because I was frightened because I had all these pictures in my head because I had been watching *Mayberry* [a drama series about a psychiatrist]. I knew that inside these places weren't very nice and it's not actually a bad series but I had two appointments and I ran away from both of them.

The media have certainly contributed to the stigma associated with mental illness. In the course of this study, mental health workers described to us how people mask their symptoms for years with drink or drugs because they would rather be seen as a 'drunken bampot' than risk being defined as mentally ill. Paradoxically, one user described to us how he had first sought help because he was afraid that he was becoming 'like the mad people (he) had read about'. He described how his understanding of mental illness had largely relied on media images:

> The image I had was of violence – the image of madmen, idiots and loonies, the people I used to laugh about ... Myra Hindley and Ian Brady that was my image of mad people ... from the London press where I lived at the time, down in London ... and I had also seen men in a hospital dressed in suits and fighting with brollies (while passing on a train).

This understanding had then changed with his direct experience. His first response on arriving at hospital was 'no, no this is for crazy people, I shouldn't be here'. But then, 'when I spoke to them I thought they were all right'. His experience also shows some of the range of sources which can inform opinion and belief. Another group member described how her experiences as a child had affected her responses. Her foster father was head gardener in a psychiatric hospital: 'When I was nine years old I used to go round with him in the grounds ... I quite honestly used to feel at ease with the patients, it was like a protectiveness with the patients, there was no fear there.' She also pointed to the distress caused by lurid headlines about psychotics and killings. In this, she raised another dimension to the potential impact of media on some users of services. She expressed the fear that lurid coverage might trigger people who are 'going through a difficult time to lash out'. She commented that: 'It could so easily trigger people off if there's a lot of anger and resentment and confusion and pent-up feelings.'
This was in fact how she had felt:

> That doctor in hospital had said to me 'Have you read the news, have you seen the TV?' (about a particular case) and there was an anger in me for saying that because I thought, God he knows how I am feeling ... He was a very understanding doctor. I think at the time what he was trying to say to me was 'if you feel like that come and tell us'.

This is an important point which has been very little discussed. But it certainly raises the issue that a lurid and violence-focused media not only misrepresents the actual nature of most mental distress, but could also act to promote harmful behaviour in some people.
Not all media output was perceived as negative. The programme *Takin' Over the Asylum* (BBC) was praised. The characters in this drama were sometimes distressed but were also shown as witty, proud and capable. One group member spoke of the soap opera *Coronation Street* and the featuring of one of its characters as suffering from depression. This had a very positive effect:

> (The media) can have a good effect. I suffer from depression and my mother who is a great *Coronation Street* fan watched Emily, she got depressed and I think ended up in hospital. I don't know how accurate it was but my mother understood a lot more about what I'd been going through for the past eight or ten years after that, 'oh it can't be that embarrassing because Emily had it'.

But another group drew attention to the possible negative effects of soap opera portrayals. Because of the nature of storylines and the swift turnover of plots, characters can move in and out of 'problems' very quickly. One group discussed the potential negative effects of this:

> First speaker: That Paul in *Neighbours* – he had a nervous breakdown he was catatonic. He went away for a couple of weeks holiday and then he was better. When I was really ill – I would watch and I'd think, what am I doing wrong, why aren't I getting better?
>
> Second speaker: It's giving people false hope.
>
> First speaker: It gives a false impression of the illness itself.
>
> Third speaker: Even a relative might say – 'look, on *Neighbours* they're getting better, why aren't you?'

The most powerful negative effect seemed to be in the area of self-definition and the stigma developed and reinforced by media portrayals. As one group member put it, 'You see a programme and it shows a very bad image of what it feels like yourself and then you think "what are my neighbours going to think about it?".' Another group member described to us in detail his feelings when he was given the label of being schizophrenic:

> When I was told I was schizophrenic, I was very intimidated by it – I thought I was some sort of monster. I didn't actually feel like a monster, but when they said I was schizophrenic, I just couldn't believe it ... It's just such a hell of a word, you know and it's got a hell of a stigma ... I just thought it was Jeckyll and Hyde. I was just one of those people I'm characterising this morning [for having incorrect beliefs about mental illness] ... but you're really more likely to hurt yourself – what was blasting through my head was you'll never get a job, you'll never get a sick line, you'll have nowhere to live. It was just going through my head, kill yourself.

This group member was asked about where his original ideas on mental illness had come from, He replied:

> *Jane Eyre* was my mother's favourite programme and I think I got it from her. We watched it faithfully every Saturday night. She [a character in the story] was insane and she ran around screaming and shouting and burnt the house down – and that instilled real fear in me ... They'll burn the house down, they'll stab you, they'll kill you – that's what I thought myself until I realised I had a problem myself.

He also described the changes in his social relationships: 'When my neighbours knew that I was schizophrenic, they were worried about getting into the lift with me – they didn't want to be in a confined space, and they wouldn't open the door to me.' He described what happened when his window cleaner saw tools which he kept in his flat: 'My window cleaner asked me "would you not hit me over the head with the hammer?" – I had to reassure him that, "look mate, I'm not violent" and he was telling the neighbours. It rots you, it just rots you.'

Conclusions

The stigmatisation of those who are mentally distressed has a long history in our culture and obviously predates our contemporary media. It must also be said that the portrayal of mental illness in films, on television and in the press is not the only source of public information and understanding in this area. Nonetheless, media coverage does have a very important influence. Our study in this volume of the content of press and television showed that two-thirds of media references to mental health related to violence and that these negative images tended to receive 'headline' treatment while more positive items were largely 'back page' in their profile, such as problem page, letters or health columns. We have also showed that this coverage had a major impact on audiences. Forty per cent of the people in the sample which we took believed that serious mental illness was associated with violence, while giving the media as the source of their beliefs. We have shown here that media images which stigmatise mental illness can also have a pervasive and damaging effect on users of services and on their immediate social relationships.

Our research also has implications for social policy. There is such a climate of ignorance and fear around the subject of mental illness that policy initiatives such as community care must be accompanied by a major public information campaign to challenge dominant images and beliefs. There have been other problems with the community care initiative relating to issues such as the level of resources which have been made available, but the fear and stigmatising effects produced by media accounts are key problems in their own right which must be addressed. The issue which confronts users of services, their carers, mental health professionals and health educators is how can this influence be changed.

Changing the media

The number of people who have periods of mental distress is very large – with 12 million people having some psychiatric problems each year and at least 300,000 thought to be 'seriously mentally ill' at any time (Utting 1994). But the key issue here is the gap between this experience and the manner in which mental illness is so often portrayed in media accounts. This was recently discussed in an addition of the Radio 4 programme *All in the Mind*. As one contributor noted: ' "Psycho" or "looney" or "psycho sex fiend", these kinds of phrases are very sensationalist and are not representative of my condition.' Another contributor took up the same theme:

> I have a diagnoses of schizophrenia and I am just a normal decent law-abiding citizen, non-violent and I just try to get on with my life as best I can within the community and these attacks by the press on me are not helping me to do that. (BBC Radio 4, 18 April 1995)

The media stereotypes and the stigma which they carry distort a fundamental truth about mental distress as experienced by very many people. As David King recently put it: 'It's a human condition, you can experience, you can recover and you can resume normally functioning' (King 1995). At present, there are many attempts being made by users of services, mental health professionals and some journalists to produce a more informed media coverage. In Manchester, the Schizophrenia Media Agency provide themselves as speakers for television and radio programmes. By their presence as 'declared' schizophrenics they challenge the prevailing images. In other words they appear as rather 'ordinary' people rather than as the monsters of popular media accounts.

In April 1995, three thousand psychiatrists signed a petition which criticised media coverage of mental illness, citing the research undertaken by the Glasgow Media Group. The petition was sent to the editors of the national press and the controllers of BBC, ITV and Channel 4 television. Its text was as follows:

1 We, fellows and members of the Royal College of Psychiatrists are seriously concerned at the existence of persistently inaccurate media presentations of mental illness.
2 We note the existence of recent research which has shown the wide-spread use by the media of stigmatising images of mental illness and that these portrayals have a negative impact on public beliefs and attitudes to people suffering from psychiatric ill-health.
3 The experience of doctors and others working in this area is that such images have a damaging effect on psychologically distressed individuals, their families and carers. These images can adversely affect self esteem and confidence. They increase the fear of psychiatric illness amongst families and within society as a whole and make processes for seeking help and recovery more difficult.
4 We call for a major debate to take place particularly within the media, within broadcasting and the press, to question the persistent replication of stigmatising and false images of psychiatric illness. We request the broadcasting authorities to encourage the making of programmes which give a fair and accurate account of mental health issues. We ask that the broadcasting and print industries produce codes of conduct to guide journalists in this area.

The demands for a code of practice for journalists, and for programmes to be made exploring these issues, are especially important. The launch of the petition was a significant moment in a long struggle to change the media. This struggle is equivalent in some ways to the demands to end racism and homophobia in the press and television. When it was first said that programmes such as the *Black and White Minstrel Show* were racist, it was regarded by some as being an eccentric or extreme view of what was 'normal' television. One member of our interview groups commented on how 'normal' it still is to laugh about mental illness:

Have you seen the new advert for radio rentals? The thing is it's 'don't be a rental case' which is a pun on mental case. It's a man on a rocking chair, in a white room, bulging eyes. Now if some copywriter in an ad agency had come up with a play between Lucozade and AIDS and shown an AIDS patient dying it wouldn't have been allowed, the IBA would have stopped it, the Advertising Standards would have stopped it. No commissioning editor would have allowed it to be shown.

Those who make media products can be made more aware of the problems that they are creating. But the demands for change cannot be left simply to mental health professionals. Users of mental health services, their families and supporters should all be actively involved. This can be achieved by organising special groups to deal with media issues within existing organisations for users. These media groups can then contribute on a regular basis to press and television and can criticise and comment on particular representations. They can apply for access to television and radio to make their own programmes. They can also write directly to the controllers of television and newspaper editors asking what progress has been made on guidelines for journalists and in changing the dominant images. In this they can seek the support of local MPs and other public figures who can write jointly with them. The media will not change until there is a movement which demands it.

References

Appleby, L. and Wessely, S. (1988) 'Public attitudes to mental illness: the influence of the Hungerford massacre', *Medicine, Science and the Law*, **28** (4): 291–95.

Atkinson, J. M. and Coia, D. A. (1995) 'Families coping with schizophrenia: a model of group work for family support', in Willey, J. (ed.) *Families Coping with Schizophrenia*, Wiley, Chichester.

Barry, M. (1993) 'Community mental health care: promoting a better quality of life for long-term clients', in D. Trent and C. Reed (eds) *Promoting Mental Health*, vol. 2, Avebury, Aldershot.

Belson, W. (1967) 'A study of some of the effects of viewing programs in the television series *The Hurt Mind*', in W. A. Belson (ed.) *The Impact of Television: Methods and Findings in Program Research*, Crosby Lockwood and Son Ltd., London.

Birch, J. (1991) 'Towards the restoration of traditional values in the psychiatry of schizophrenia', *Context*, **8**: 21–26.

Broadcasting Standards Council (1994) *A Code of Practice*, 2nd edn., Broadcasting Standards Council, London.

Brockington, I., Hall, P., Levings, J. and Murphy, C. (1993) 'The community's tolerance of the mentally ill', *British Journal of Psychiatry*, **162**: 93–99.

Brockman, J., D'Arcy, C. and Edmonds, L. (1979) 'Facts or artifacts? Changing public attitudes toward the mentally ill', *Social Science and Medicine*, **13A**: 673–82.

Community Care (1993) 'New attack on services', *Community Care*, 12 August: 1.

Confidential Inquiry (1994) *A Preliminary Report on Homicide*, London, Steering Committee.

Day, D. and Page, S. (1986) 'Portrayal of mental illness in Canadian newspapers', *Canadian Journal of Psychiatry*, **31** (December): 813–17.

Department of Health (1989) *Caring for People. Community Care in the next Decade and Beyond.* HMSO, London.

Department of Health (1992) *The Health of the Nation: A Strategy for Health in England*, Department of Health, London.

Department of Health (1993a) *The Health of the Nation Key Area Handbook: Mental Illness*, Department of Health, London.

Department of Health (1993b) *Attitudes to Mental Illness*, Department of Health, London.

Domino, G. (1983) 'Impact of the film *One Flew Over the Cuckoo's Nest* on attitudes to mental illness', *Psychological Reports*, 53: 179–182.

Forrest, S. (1992) 'Hospital and Community: clients' and carers' experience of life in two residential settings for the mentally ill,' M.Phil thesis, University of Edinburgh.

Goldacre, M., Seagroatt, V. and Hawton, K. (1993) 'Suicide after discharge from psychiatric inpatient care', *The Lancet*, 342 (31 July): 283–86.

Hall, P., Brockington, I., Levings, J. and Murphy, C. (1993) 'A comparison of responses to the mentally ill in two communities', *British Journal of Psychiatry*, 162: 99–108.

Health Service Journal (1992) 'Neighbours threaten care home bid', *Health Service Journal*, 5 November: 6.

Henderson, L (1996) 'Incest in *Brookside*: Audience responses to the Jordache story', Channel 4, London.

Huxley, P. (1993) 'Location and stigma: a survey of community attitudes to mental illness – Part 1. Enlightenment and stigma', *Journal of Mental Health*, 2: 73–80.

Hyler, S. *et al.* (1991) 'Homicidal maniacs and narcissistic parasites: stigmatisation of mentally ill persons in the movies', *Hospital and Community Psychiatry*, 42 (10).

King, D. (1995) 'Prevention – lessons learned from task force experiences', unpublished conference paper, Mental Health Promotion Seminar, March 1995, Plymouth and Torbay Health Authority.

Kitzinger, J. (1993) 'Media messages and what people know about Acquired Immune Deficiency Syndrome' in Glasgow University Media Group (eds) *Getting the Message*, Routledge, London.

Kubey, R. (1996) 'On not finding media effects: conceptual problems in the notion of an "active audience", in L. Gronberg, J. Hay and E. Mortello (eds) *Towards a Comprehensive Theory of the Audience*, Westview Press, Boulder, Colorado.

Liebs, T. and Katz, E. (1990) *The Export of Meaning: Cross Cultural Readings of 'Dallas'*. Oxford University Press. New York.

Lull, J. (1988) *World Families Watch Television*, Sage, Newbury, California.

McCollam, A. (1992) *Community Care Planning for Mental Health in Scotland*, Scottish Association for Mental Health, Edinburgh.

MacLean, U. (1969) 'Community attitudes to mental illness in Edinburgh', *British Journal of Preventive and Social Medicine*, 23: 45–52.

Melzer, H., Baljit, G. and Petticrew, M. (1994) *The prevalence of psychiatric morbidity amongst adults aged 16–64 living in private households in Great Britain*, OPCS Survey of Psychiatric Morbidity Bulletin No. 1, Office of Population Censuses and Surveys, London.

Mental Health Act Commission (1993) *Fifth Biennial Report*, HMSO, London.

Mental Welfare Commission for Scotland (1994) *Annual Report 1993–1994*, Mental Welfare Commission for Scotland, Edinburgh.

Miller, D. *et al.* (1992) 'Message misunderstood', *Times Higher Education Supplement*, July 3: 18.

Monahan, J. (1992) 'Mental disorder and violent behaviour – perceptions and evidence', *American Psychologist*, 41 (4): 511–21.

MORI (1979) *Public Attitudes to Mental Illness*, Market and Opinion Research International, London.

Morley, D. (1986) *Family Television*. Comedia/Routledge, London.

Petch, A. (1990) *Heaven Compared to a Hospital Ward*, Social Work Research Centre, University of Stirling.

Philo, G. (1990) *Seeing and Believing: The Influence of Television*, Routlege, London.

Philo, G., Henderson, L and McLaughlin, G (1993) *Mass Media Representations of Mental Health and Illness: Content Study*, Glasgow Media Group/Health Education Board for Scotland, Glasgow Media Group, Glasgow.

Potter, J. and Wetherell, M. (1987) *Discourse and Social Psychology: Beyond Attitudes and Behaviour*, London, Sage.

Powell, J. (1993) 'Changing patterns of mental healthcare: the role of support staff in developing local services', in D. Trent and C. Reed (eds) *Promoting Mental Health*, vol. 2, Avebury, Aldershot.

Royal College of Psychiatrists (1995) *Attitudes Towards Depression*, Royal College of Psychiatrists, London.

Sayce, L. (1995a) 'An ill wind in a climate of fear', *The Guardian* (Society), January 18: 6–7.

Sayce, L. (1995b) 'Response to violence: a framework for fair treatment' in Crichton, J. (ed.) *Psychiatric Patient Violence, Risk and Response*, Duckworth, London.

Scottish Affairs Committee (1995) *Closure of Psychiatric Hospitals in Scotland*, vol. 1, HMSO, London.

Scottish Association for Mental Health (1992) *Anti-discrimination Legislation for Disabled People*, Scottish Association for Mental Health, Edinburgh.

Scottish Mental Health Forum (1992) *Community Care and Consultation*, Scottish Association for Mental Health, Edinburgh.

Scottish Office (1991) *Health Education in Scotland: A National Policy Statement*, Scottish Office, Home and Health Department, Edinburgh.

Scottish Office (1995) *Priorities and planning guidance for the NHS in Scotland 1996/7*, Management Executive letter (1995) 51, NHS Management Executive, Edinburgh.

Signorielli, N. (1989) 'The stigma of mental illness on television', *Journal of Broadcasting and Electronic Media*, 33 (3): 325–31.

Simic, P., Gilfillan, S. and O'Donnell, O. (1992) *A Study of the Rehabilitation and Discharge of Long-term Psychiatric Patients from the Royal Edinburgh Hospital*, Social Work Research Centre, University of Stirling.

Steadman, H. and Cocozza, J. (1977) 'Selective reporting and the public's misconceptions of the criminally insane', *Public Opinion Quarterly*, 41 (Winter): 523–33.

Steering Committee of the Confidential Inquiry into Homicides and Suicides by Mentally Ill People (1996) *Report of the Confidential Inquiry into Homicides and Suicides by Mentally Ill People,* Royal College of Psychiatrists, London.

Thornicroft, G., Gooch, C. and Dayson, D. (1992) 'The TAPS project 17: readmissions to hospital for long-term psychiatric patients after discharge in the community', *British Medical Journal,* **305**: 996–998.

Utting, W. (1994) *Creating Community Care. Report of Mental Health Foundation Inquiry into Community Care for People with Severe Mental Illness.* The Mental Health Foundation, London.

Vousden, M. (1989) 'Loony lefties and mad mullahs', *Nursing Times,* **85** (28): 16–17.

Wahl, O. and Lefkowits, J. (1989) 'Impact of a television film on attitudes towards mental illness', *American Journal of Community Psychology,* **17** (4): 521–28.

WHO (1991) *Targets for Health for All: The Health Policy for Europe,* World Health Organisation, Regional Office for Europe, Copenhagen.

Wilkinson, G. (1994) 'Can suicide be prevented?', *British Medical Journal,* **309**: 860–61.

Wober, J. (1989) *Healthy Minds on Healthy Airwaves: Effects of Channel 4's 1986 Mental Health Programme Campaign,* Independent Broadcasting Authority Research Department, London.

Wober, J. (1991) *Television and Mental Ill Health,* Independent Television Commission Research Department, London.

Appendix 1

Words and phrases associated with mental health/illness in the media

Anxiety
Apocalyptic attitude (David Koresh)
Around the twist
Amphetamine psychosis

Bampot
Barking mad
Barmy
Barmy boroughs
Barmy Brent (Council)
Basket case
Batty
Bedlam
Berserk
Bestial
Bonkers
Brainwashed

Compulsion
(He) Cooks your brains
(He'll) Crack up
Crackers
Crackpot
Crazy
Crazed

Daft
Deluded
Demented

Dementia
Depraved
Depression
Deranged
Disturbed
Dotty

Egomania
Euro-nutter (Jacques Delors)

Fanatics
Fetish
Few sandwiches short of a picnic, a
Fiend
Fighting mad
Flipped her lid
Freaks
Frenzied knifeman
Funny farm
Funny turn, having a

Ga-ga
Guilt-induction (Cults)

Headcase
Head examined, I must need my
Hopelessly neurotic
Hypochondriac
Hysteria
Hysterical

Insane

Jerusalem Syndrome (When person believes he/she is reincarnation of biblical figure)

Loony
Loony bin
Loony doctor
Loony tune, Mr
Lost her marbles
Lost her senses
Lunatic

Mad, going
Mad as hatter
Madcap
Madness, method in your
Mad dog
Mad-eyed courage (to go out and win)
Mad house
Mad man
Mad rush
Mania
Maniac
Manic-depressive
Manic-depressive psychosis
Masochistic obsession
Mass suicide pact
Menace to society
Mental
Mental, chucking a
Mental breakdown
Mental health, you've ruined my
Mental turmoil
Mentally competent
Mentally zapped (Brainwashed)
Mind, I'm losing my
Mindless
Mind-blowing
Mind-control
Monster
Motorway madness

Nervous breakdown
Nervous disorder

Neurotic
Neurotically charged
Not the full shilling
Not very well in the head
Nut-bin
Nutcase
Nuts
Nutter
Nymphomaniac

Obsessed, completely
Obsessive,
Off his cake
Off his rocker
Out of their Neanderthal skulls

Paranoia
Paranoia, fits of
Paranoiac nut
Pathological lying
Pervert
Phobia
Post-natal depression
Post-traumatic stress disorder
Potty
Power-crazy
Psychiatric help, need
Psycho-babble (Psycholinguistic jargon)
Psycho-cannibal
Pyscho-killer
Psychological warfare
Psychologically disturbed
Psycho
Psychopath
Psychopathic maniac
Psychosomatic (Illnesses)
Psychotherapy
Psychotic

Raving Right (as opposed to 'Loony Left')
Reactive psychosis
Relatively sane

Sadistic
Schizophrenia
Schizophrenic (urban) sprawl
Screw loose, he's got a

Screwball

Self-revulsion

Sex-crazed

Sex-mad

Sex maniac

Sexual delusion

Shrinks

Sick

Sicko

Sinister

Soccer nut

Soft in the head

Squander-mania

Stark staring mad

Stark staring bonkers

Stir-crazy

Suicide

Suicidal

Top himself, he tried to

Unpredictable (David Koresh)

Unstable

Wacko

Wacky

Warped

Water lunacy (Privatization)

Weirdo

Wild-eyed

Zany

Zealots (Cult members)

Appendix 2

Newspaper extracts

SET ON FIRE

Hunt for fiend who tried to burn the face off Derek, 7

POLICE ARE TODAY LOOKING FOR THE EVIL MANIAC WHO TRIED TO DISFIGURE THIS INNOCENT CHILD WHAT KIND OF WORLD DO WE ALIVE IN WHEN A CHILD CANT EVEN BE ALOWED TO PLAY IN THE STREET

THE VICTIM: Schoolboy Derek Cripps . . . his face was badly burned by searing flames

BY A MANIAC

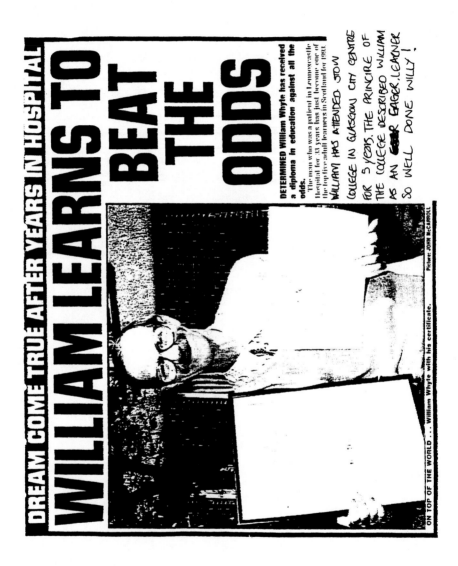

DREAM COME TRUE AFTER YEARS IN HOSPITAL

WILLIAM LEARNS TO BEAT THE ODDS

DETERMINED William Whyte has received a diploma in education against all the odds.

The man who was a patient in Lennoxcastle Hospital for 33 years has just become one of the top five adult learners in Scotland for 1993.

ON TOP OF THE WORLD ... William Whyte with his certificate.   Picture: JOHN McCARROLL

WILLIAM WAS PROBABLY ADMITTED TO THIS MENTAL HOME AND PROBABLY WASN'T MENTALY ILL — AND HE WAS A JUST A VICTEM OF SIRCUMSTAINCES.

PSYCHO FAN STALKS CINDY

Stunning Model Cindy Crawford, married to Hollywood Superstar Richard Gere, revealed at a press conference today that she had been the victim of a crazed psychopath who had been stalking her for some time. The besotted fan had been pestering Cindy with obscene phone calls over recent months. With the help of the police, Cindy arranged to meet the sick intruder and he is awaiting trial.

TERRIFIED: Cindy set up a meeting to trap the sick intruder

PSYCHO FAN STALKS CINDY

Supermodel Cindy Crawford, wife of Hollywood star Richard Gere has revealed the fact that she months ago has been living in fear of attack by an obsessed fan who has been making terrifying threats.

The fan who identifies with Norman Bates in director Alfred Hitccock's box office smash hit "Psycho" has been writing and telephoning Cindy as well as sending her bizarre and frightening packages. Mindful of the fate of other personalities who has suffered similar threats Cindy is cooperating with the police to attempt to identify the sick pervert.

Cindy once filmed video was seen a major American news programme for stars, Book Skellett and Dierdre Austen John as ...

TERRIFIED: Cindy set up a meeting to trap the sick intruder

Victim of Clair Burne.

In an interview Cindy said "these people need help. He will have to be found before he can do any more harm. I am doing all I can to help identify him."

1 Dean + Young
C Coker Cool

A. Young

Index